the Gathering Place

the Gathering Place

EMPOWERING YOUR COMMUNITY
THROUGH URBAN CHURCH EDUCATION

James R. Love Sr.

GRAND RAPIDS, MICHIGAN 49530 USA

We want to hear from you. Please send your comments about this book to us in care of the address below. Thank you.

GRAND RAPIDS, MICHIGAN 49530 USA

WWW.ZONDERVAN.COM

ZONDERVAN™

The Gathering Place
Copyright © 2002 by James R. Love Sr.

Requests for information should be addressed to:

Zondervan, *Grand Rapids, Michigan 49530*

Library of Congress Cataloging-in-Publication Data

Love, James R., 1956–
    The gathering place : empowering your community through urban church education / James R. Love Sr.
      p. cm.
    Includes bibliographical references.
    ISBN 0-310-24140-5
    1. African American churches. 2. Christian education. 3. City churches. 4. Church and social problems — United States. I. Title.
BR563.N4 L65 2002
268'.089'96073 — dc21   2002008989

All Scripture quotations, unless otherwise indicated, are from the King James Version of the Bible. NKJV indicates the *Holy Bible, New King James Version,* copyright © 1982 by Thomas Nelson, Inc. NASB indicates the *New American Standard Bible,* copyright © 1960, 1962, 1963, 1968, 1971, 1972, 1973, 1975, 1977, 1995 by the Lockman Foundation, La Habra, California.

Interior design by Tracey Moran

Printed in the United States of America

---

02 03 04 05 06 07 08 /❖ DC/ 10 9 8 7 6 5 4 3 2 1

To the Right Reverend John L. Meares,
who encouraged me to pursue the academic
and intellectual dimension of my nature
while staying grounded in the Holy Scriptures.

To the late Dr. Harvie Conn,
my Doctorate of Ministry advisor,
who cultivated in me a passion for urban ministry
and inspired me to write this book.

Contents

Acknowledgments

There are scores of people I would like to thank in this undertaking. For me to even contemplate writing a book is beyond my wildest imagination. I recall one day back in 1990 when I went to eat lunch at a McDonald's near the church. I happened to get into a conversation with a homeless man. I guessed he was in his late forties, and he was very disheveled in appearance. But I felt compelled to invite him to have lunch with me. I learned a lot that afternoon.

This man felt that the church never seemed to really be very concerned about the poor or needy. He said they only paid lip service to helping "people like me." Further, he said he wished there were more educational programs to give him the confidence and training he needed to rise above his present circumstances. His words got to my heart. So, to that forgotten homeless person who grounded a young and idealistic preacher in truth and reality, I say thank you.

To Veda Whittelsey, who typed my Doctorate of Ministry project—which contained many of the concepts contained in this book—thank you.

To Minister LaDorothy Pittman, who has done a yeoman's job of typing and retyping the early manuscripts, thank you.

To Dr. Joseph Durham, who read and provided helpful suggestions in the early drafts of the manuscript, thanks.

To my loving wife, Deborah, who is my number one fan and number one critic, thanks for allowing me time to write when I know you wanted more time with me. I love you!

CHAPTER 1

Introduction

Forging a Vision

I was in seminary in the late 1980s when I began to take my call as a preacher and Christian educator seriously. I was particularly interested in how urban churches handle the relationship between Christian education and social challenges. I discovered that because cities are usually heavily populated, most urban churches are confronted daily with the poor, the homeless, winos, and welfare-dependent mothers. I wondered whether there was more the church could do to help these people whom society had tossed away. I saw urban ministries organizing Meals on Wheels, soup kitchens, or clothing banks—all programs that I call "handout ministries."

At the same time, I was studying Black Theology, a type of theology that emphasizes liberation. That caused me to think about the connections between education and empowerment, and between empowerment and liberation. As I started on my journey to discover what urban church education is and to contemplate how it relates to empowerment, I was soundly disappointed. I discovered that very little work had been done in this area. Aside from the works of Donald B. Rogers, Cullen Brichett, and Olivia Pearl Stokes, most of what I discovered about urban church education also had to do with "handout ministry." So I began to wonder what could be done to give the poor and the oppressed a "hand up." I firmly believe that education equals liberation for the poor and oppressed.

In 1983 I was hired by Evangel Temple, a large, urban, African-American church in Washington, D.C. My job was to lead its education ministry and develop a Bible institute. Moreover, I have taught workshops and offered seminars on Christian education within an urban context. Therefore this book is the culmination of my experience interacting with churches in cities from around the country.

My basic assumption in writing this book is that far too many black independent churches regard Christian education as a desirable goal but typically give little or no financial resources to achieve it. Education sometimes seems to be just an afterthought. In most settings, the person who coordinates the education ministry and the people who teach are essentially very willing workers but come to the task with little or no training in the basic methodologies of education. Furthermore, they are then offered little training , so they must simply do the best they can to keep children, youth, or adults entertained until the church service starts at 11 A.M.

For too many pastors, Christian education is reduced to Vacation Bible School in July or to Sunday school quarterly curricula materials year-round. In contrast, these same churches have music ministries staffed by someone who has at least a basic level of competency. The result is that too many churches are musically dynamic but educationally static. This may be a reason why studies done by George Barna and George Gallup have shown that among people who identify themselves as Christians, the level of Bible knowledge is very low. I believe that if this trend continues, a generation of illiterate Christians will emerge.

I see urban church education as a powerful tool for meeting these needs and overcoming these past shortcomings. Urban church education is an effective vehicle for the empowerment of African-Americans and other ethnic minorities who are socially oppressed. Without adequate skills or the appropriate knowledge in this "communication age," the poor and the underclass have little chance of getting ahead. I believe that the urban church must step into the educational void left by public schools. The urban church must become the citadel of learning and empowerment within the neighborhood. This empowerment releases those who are disenfranchised, oppressed, and powerless. This release is accomplished through urban church educational principles. These educational principles utilize the liberating power of the gospel. And this liberating power affects the spiritual, political, and economic situation of the marginalized.

The problem is that black churches in the urban situation have only seen the models of handout ministry. They have not seen the powerful hand-up potential that lies in urban church education. Therefore Christian education must be expanded to include programs with a Christian worldview that motivate and inspire people to achieve. This will ultimately result in empowerment. Urban church education can empower the oppressed to obtain what has been denied them: the freedom that comes through knowledge.

In this book I present both the theory of urban church education and various ways in which it finds practical expression. That is, my intention is to provide a resource book that can and will be used by churches in urban areas. This book serves as a training manual for the people responsible for organizing education programs in their local church. It offers some valuable guidance to those who are ill-equipped for or overwhelmed by the task of urban church education.

In writing this book, I have decided to use an inductive approach instead of the usual deductive approach. The inductive approach starts out with the setting and then moves toward developing certain theories. By contrast, the deductive approach starts out with developing theories and then moves to the setting. Both of these are legitimate ways of thinking, but an inductive line of thinking better reflects my own experience. I have observed the urban scene both through my experiences and by interacting with others who were in a similar setting. Afterward, I began thinking critically about my experiences, and in doing so, I observed certain patterns and principles that are reflected here.

Therefore, chapter 2 explores what urban church education is and explains some of the characteristics and principles we find at its foundation. Chapter 3 examines the context for urban church education, as I make some personal observations about the city and what distinguishes it from other social environments. Chapter 4 defines empowerment and examines how empowerment principles can be used in urban church education.

Chapter 5 reflects on my experience at Evangel Temple—specifically, how we structured our educational programs to empower people. Chapter 6 is a basic introduction to educational and teaching methods, an understanding of which, as I have noted, far too many urban church educators lack.

Chapter 7 offers a summary of the struggle for education for African-Americans from the era of slavery, through Reconstruction, up to the landmark *Brown vs. Board of Education* decision of the U.S. Supreme Court in 1954. This is helpful because this struggle is part of the context for the vision shared in this book.

Finally, chapter 8 is a brief look at various philosophical systems that compete for the minds of urban dwellers.

Each chapter ends with a summary and several provocative discussion questions.

In between the chapters are case studies of local churches and church organizations that have established various kinds of empowerment programs with some success.

CHAPTER 2

Empowerment

Why Urban Church Education Is Needed

Urban church education is a fairly unknown topic in the dia-logue of urban ministries. In fact, to the general observer there would seem to be little or no relationship between the two. Some would argue that the term *urban church* refers to how a church functions in the inner-city context as compared with a church in a suburban or rural community. And differences are obvious. The inner-city church is confronted with overwhelming prob-lems such as poverty, homelessness, and drugs. Often the church is understaffed and lacks adequate resources to minister effec-tively in its environment. The gospel mandate of declaring the kingdom of God as a kingdom of justice and righteousness seems unrealistic to an inner-city church.

Yet the urban church is called to be faithful in its ministry of manifesting that kingdom of God within the city. Jesus emphat-ically stated that the poor must have the Good News preached to them (Luke 4:18). The fact is that the poor are abundant in the city!

In contrast, some would argue that education is instruction that occurs within a certain kind of institution devoted to that purpose, such as a school. Therefore, education is not a signifi-cant tool of urban ministry. I believe, however, that education is

an effective and essential tool for change and empowerment—
that is, giving people both the spirit and the opportunities needed
to achieve a better way of life. The church can step up to provide
education where suffering public schools have failed. Education
and skill development equal empowerment and liberation.

This chapter therefore address two critical questions: What is
urban church education? And what is empowerment?

Defining Urban Church Education

Urban church education is an approach to education that
embraces the principles of empowering people to become achievers. This approach is founded on equipping people for success in
skilled vocational or academic areas. Also, it is unique to the
urban setting, and it is a response to the peculiar challenges of
the urban situation: homelessness, poverty, injustice, crime, and
drugs. Urban church education has a mind-set that is pragmatic
in its basic philosophy; it says that whatever it takes to empower
people to improve their situation in life will be done. It reaches
out to the working poor, those who live in housing projects, and
those on welfare with programs that encourage, uplift, and provide practical "how-tos" for improving their situation.

Moreover, urban church education is the body of Christ—
the church—reaching out beyond its four walls and touching the
neighborhood with the healing hands of an incarnate Jesus
Christ. It is contextual; it is concerned with properly analyzing
the neighborhood, assessing the needs, and responding accord-
ingly with empowerment programs. Urban church education is
sensitive to the culture of the community.

For example, a neighborhood that is largely Hispanic is different from one that is largely African-American. Most pastors
know how important biblical exegesis is to preparing sermons;
they want to be careful that they properly interpret God's Word
so their hearers can understand. Similarly, the church must properly exegete the surrounding neighborhood; a good analysis will
help the church be sensitive and responsive to the culture.

In defining urban church education we must consider its foundations. First and foremost, urban church education is Christian. It must be theologically orthodox regarding the essential tenets of the Christian faith. It rejects non-Christian education as humanistic or man-centered. Professor Cornelius Van Til made this cogent point: "Non-Christian education is Godless education. Godless education ignores or denies that man was created responsible to God."[1]

Second, urban church education takes an inductive approach and not the typical deductive approach. In other words, the setting determines the approach; it is not a theory developed independent from the setting. Donald B. Rogers insightfully argues that traditional educational methodology first established a theory that was then imposed upon setting. He advocates the reverse.

> This is not the usual religious education pattern of theory-to-setting in which a set of foundational ideas becomes the basis for theory which is then applied to the practice of education. Rather, use an inductive approach to theory which seeks to find theory implicit in the practice of religious education, in the setting.[2]

Rogers sees the setting-to-theory approach as the most effective for teachers on the front lines. However, he does not discard the value of the theoretician. He contends that the practitioner makes a valuable contribution to the theoretician as well as theoretician to practitioner. Both are needed. Finally, he comments,

> I see the best of both worlds, the front line practitioner and the professionally trained academician working in a dialogue of respect to address the perplexing issues of urban church education.[3]

Because the setting where urban church education occurs varies from neighborhood to neighborhood, it imposes no predetermined agenda. The local church that is sensitive to the educational needs of its neighborhood responds with programs that empower.

All this may seem vague and theoretical, but it is very important to understand what is going on here. When Rogers talks about a theory-to-setting approach, he means that the standard approach most educators take is to construct a set of theories or ideas that they hope will work in a particular setting. In contrast, a setting-to-theory approach begins by observing a specific setting, then developing theories that reflect what does or does not work there.

Let's say Holy Temple Church is located in the city, and Pastor Jenkins wants to establish a program to give elementary and middle school-age young people some constructive activities after school. Essentially, a setting-to-theory approach says, "Let's begin with the situation at hand." In this example, young kids come home from school before their parents get off work. Since the kids play in an area near the church, Pastor Jenkins organizes an after-school program that allows the kids to play, do homework, and receive tutoring in a safe environment.

Now let's suppose again that this program was effective in taking kids off the street corner. What ideas can be gleaned from this experience that can be helpful to other programs starting around the city? Do you see how the setting determines what the ideas are going to look like? Observe that the ideas are actually reflections of the setting.

Empowerment

Earlier I defined urban church education as an approach to education that embraces the principles of empowering people to become achievers. The keyword in the definition is *empowering*. To empower means to enable a person to be an achiever. Becoming an achiever begins with developing a positive self-image. Those who live in the urban situation are often bombarded by many stimuli—mostly negative—that tend to slowly destroy any self-esteem or vision for achievement. Living in a world filled with gangs and violence wears down any hope or optimism for gaining a better situation. This is why urbanites—

particularly minorities who live in the "hood," ghetto, or bar-
rios—often come across to suburbanites as having a harsh or
direct personality. Those who live in the inner city are realists
who have seen the "wages of sin" exact a psychological toll both
on their communities and on their lives.

In this situation the church must step in and provide hope
and empowerment. The city is a place that needs to feel the healing hand of Jesus Christ. This is particularly true of the poor, the
underclass, and the oppressed. The government cannot meet
both the spiritual and the physical needs of the poor. The total
needs of the poor can only be met through the body of Jesus
Christ. The urban church should be characterized by its proclamation and demonstration of empowerment for the poor. The
poor and the oppressed don't need sympathy or handouts; they
need justice, and they need to be empowered!

Robert Linthicum suggests that the poor can be empowered
through community organization. He identifies three responses
the church can give to community development. The first
response is the church picturing itself as merely being in the
city and in its neighborhood.[4] Linthicum suggests that many
churches see themselves as "in" but not "of" their neighborhood.
These churches have a physical presence but have no particular
relationship with the people around them. If the church is to provide the light of hope, it must actively engage the community
with both presence and involvement.

The second response is for a body of believers to see itself as
a church to the city and to its neighborhood.[5] This church is
active in its neighborhood. This activity may be to provide a food
bank or clothing store to meet physical needs. However, the critical flaw in this approach is that the church makes all the decisions as to what best meets the needs of its neighbors. Without
local involvement in decisions, this approach will be difficult to
maintain and will eventually collapse.

The third response is for a church to realize its role in the city
and its neighborhood.[6] This response is an "incarnational"
response. Here the church goes beyond establishing a physical

presence or being proactive in the community. Rather, it becomes the flesh and blood of the community. In other words, the church has become identified with the neighborhood. Now the people who live in the neighborhood view the church as the center of community life.

In this approach, the community plays a part in making the decisions for the church's outreach programs. The result is that people who do not attend church may begin to see a need to attend; the church is theirs, whether they attend or not. The church may structure a community board that provides directions for neighborhood outreach. (This is the idea behind a Community Development Corporation, or CDC.) The board would consist mostly of people who live in the neighborhood. A wonderful result of this is networking, coalition building, and trust being established with the city government and other municipal authorities.

However, one of the challenges that must be faced with community representation is the troubling question of what to do when members of the community do not embrace or understand a Christian orientation. I do not believe there are any easy answers to this question. The reality is that within the urban context many cultures live within blocks of one another, and multiculturalism must be acknowledged. I recommend that the essential core beliefs, morals, and ethical values be established from the outset. My own feeling is that most non-Christians are more interested in the benefits of a program that meets the real needs of the community than the doctrinal position of the church.

The church that lies within the crucible of urbanization must never shirk from its responsibility to be a source of empowerment. Although the problems may seem insurmountable, we must not and need not be discouraged. As Roger Greenway says,

> Without question, far-reaching and highly interrelated solutions have to be found that will reorder urban life at all levels. That is what urban missions is all about.[7]

Summary

In this chapter I have advocated combining two separate disciplines, urban ministry and Christian education, into one called urban church education. The goal of urban church education is empowering people to become and function as achievers. Urban church education is confronted with different situations and problems from those commonly found in suburban or rural areas, therefore at its heart it is empowerment. The poor and the underclass need more than handout ministry. They need to be empowered with hand-up ministry—which is what urban church education is all about. Finally, the church needs to have an "incarnational response," becoming virtually the flesh and blood of the community by being deeply involved in community development.

Questions for Discussion

1. How would you define *empowerment?*
2. How does the author define urban church education? Do you think such a definition is adequate? Why or why not?
3. What are the distinguishing characteristics of urban church education?
4. The author states that urban church education begins by reflecting on the particular setting or urban context and then developing the theory and programs to meet the situations. What do you see as the shortcomings and strengths of this approach?
5. Do you think that education can be an effective tool for empowering the poor and underclass? Explain.

An After-School Program

Wayne Robinson is a 6-foot-10 former NBA basketball player who also spent some time overseas in Spain playing professionally. But basketball is not what inspires Robinson. What inspires him is his vision for young adults. He noticed that in Greensboro, North Carolina, where he lives, there are very few after-school programs for the youth he felt so passionately about. He says, "I believe the Lord is leading me to establish one that has a Christian emphasis."[8] Robinson wants to empower young people to be able to make positive decisions and choices in their lives. He believes that with the gospel, a solid academic program, and mentoring, young people will be better prepared to make good life decisions.

Because of this vision, Robinson started an after-school program called the Center for Champions. In his vision statement for the Center for Champions, he makes the following analogy:

> In many ways, the youth of today are crying out—without a torch, the path to success is hard to see, especially through the tears. These youth carry the torch of tomorrow, but first they must be prepared. Love opens doors towards faith and trust. Sharing leads to better communication. Hard work results in productivity. The torch must be passed; but are these youth ready to receive it? Our vision is to prepare them to accept the torch by instilling in them the importance of love, sharing, and hard work.[9]

Robinson believes that young people are not being equipped to make good sound decisions from the multitude of choices they are confronted with. He knows of the increasing level of drug use and sexual promiscuity among young people. He believes that the schools are not doing enough and that, sadly, many parents are too busy to really talk to their offspring about making good decisions.

Good decisions, according to Robinson, include instilling a biblical frame of reference: "What does God have to say about what I am about to do is something I challenge young people to think about," he said.

He believes that an effective after-school-care program can assist parents and supplement the activity of public schools to prepare young people to carry "the torch." The program was started in August 1993, with about twenty children attending. "Several areas of concern surfaced, but all the concerns centered around the ability of our youth to make better decisions," Robinson said of the program's beginning.

The Center for Champions program offers four services: mentoring, tutoring, counseling, and cultural enrichment. Mentors work individually with young adults in a classroom setting, assisting in homework or other school-related projects. The tutoring provides students with help in learning general subjects such as math, science, and English. Counseling is available to all the students. The counselors work particularly with students who are in unhealthy situations at home or school. They have experience working with kids who come from broken homes or dysfunctional families, and they are able to offer loving concern.

In terms of cultural enrichment, the center seeks to expose the young adults to different career paths, arts, sports, and technology. In addition, the students are encouraged to participate in Bible study and group prayer time each day. Robinson stresses the importance of an emphasis on spirituality, which he sees as an element that is missing from the lives of many of the youth.

The after-school program has grown from twenty to approximately one hundred young adults. The staff has expanded from one (Robinson) to twelve. A ten-year-old fourth-grader, whom we will call Morgan, was placed in the program by his mother, who is divorced, because of her work schedule and because he is a strong-willed child who needs the type of structure that the Center for Champions offers. Morgan's mother observes that her son "really enjoys going to the Center, and Wayne [Robinson] is doing a fantastic job with the young kids."

This kind of program is especially important because it appears that in most urban families, both parents are working. This means many kids are left at home alone. Robinson believes that many churches can step into this void and readily provide an after-school program like that of the Center for Champions. He has helped several churches to set up similar programs.

One value of this program's approach is that it deals with several different aspects of students' lives. Young people who are involved in a positive atmosphere that fosters learning, cooperation, and self-esteem will be empowered to succeed in life.

There are weaknesses with the Center for Champions model. One is staff turnover, which disrupts the consistency these students need. Also, the vision statement could be written in more specific language than simply "Our vision is to prepare them [youth] to accept the torch by instilling in them the importance of love, sharing, and hard work." Finally, the Center for Champions has to share the facility with other organizations, although so far that has not caused scheduling conflicts.

Still, the Center for Champions remains an excellent model for the much-needed after-school program.

For additional information about the Center for Champions, contact Mrs. Elaine Johnson or Mr. Wayne Robinson, at 1900 Martin Luther King Jr. Drive, Greensboro, NC 27406, or (336) 271–2600.

CHAPTER 3

The City on a Hill

The Context of Urban Church Education

In discussing urban church education, it is essential to consider its context. This context is, of course, the city, or urban America. To understand this urban setting, I believe it is helpful to look at the basic differences and similarities between city and suburban-rural areas. Furthermore, I want to explore what it means to go "back to the city."

How relevant is a suburban-rural model or church ministry in a world that has been urbanized? The suburban-rural model of church ministry is still the dominant one in most people's thinking. Picture this: White picket fences, a tall church steeple, and pristine flower beds as the church sits nestled in a rural garden of Eden. This image is a caricature of the suburban-rural model, true, but even though it is exaggerated, it still influences church ministry. This model of church prevails because for too many decades the city was seen as evil, decadent, decaying, and absent of moral goodness. People thought the city was declining in population, especially by the 1950s as suburban growth mushroomed and the rise of mass transportation and expressways gave people the option to flee the city.

Today, however, the city is an important place for ministry because of the urbanization—the process by which rural areas are transformed into urban areas[1]—that has occurred all over the world. Larry Rose and Kirk Hadaway point out that

> the massive growth of the world's population in recent years has spawned cities larger than have ever existed. The cities of the world are growing at a rate that is twice that of the world's population. As a consequence, the world is rapidly becoming urban.[2]

Back to the City

To compare cities and rural-suburban areas, we first need to have a general working definition of the city. Many attempts have been made to define the city. The classic definition by Louis Wirth in his 1938 essay, "Urbanism as a Way of Life,"[3] essentially viewed the city in terms of size, density, and heterogeneity. Indeed, the most obvious feature to anyone who has traveled out of the countryside is a city's size. The immensity of the city, with its numerous tall buildings, large and mobile population, and sophisticated commercial centers makes it distinctive from the town or rural area. Although Wirth's definition has been severely criticized, most people continue to understand the city in this way. Wirth had a negative view of urbanization because it destroys the pristine, relational community of the town. To him the city demoralizes and fragments the individual, whereas the town is better at linking people in close relational bonds.

In more recent discussions, the city has not been viewed purely in terms of size, density, and heterogeneity, but also in terms of ecology. While size is a factor, there are also other variables and a range of cause-and-effect conditions that follow from them. This approach, Wirth says, "reminds one of the interrelated properties of life in the urban setting, and how each class of variables is related to and has implications for the other."[4] The weakness of this view is that the categories are arbitrary and the boundaries between them imprecise.

In the end, all attempts to define how the city functions are subjective because they depend on where a person stands. In other words, while many people see things Wirth's way, others

see the city as a place of power, freedom, diversity, or assimilation. Thus John Gulick says that

> cities are places of variety, tension and opportunity. They
> embody neither utopia nor anti-utopia. The reasons for con-
> spicuous conditions in them, good or bad, should be sought
> first in the cultures and regions of which they are only parts.[5]

Again, it depends on where a person stands.

Some people interpret the city in terms of freedom and creativity. In the city there are few boundaries that restrict the individual. One can pursue an assortment of activities with little or
no resistance. For example, the city offers a variety of job opportunities for those interested in business or government or entre-
preneurship. This freedom gives the individual a sense of
independence and autonomy. The perception of freedom and
opportunity breeds creativity. Whereas the rural community in
its sameness tends to inhibit creativity, the city tends to demand
creativity. This is seen, for example, in the arts and cultural ethos
of the city. The music styles of jazz, blues, and rap all come out
of an urban context. In sufficient variety and volume to suit anyone's tastes, artistic achievement and progress primarily come
out of the city.

However, despite the appearance of freedom and creativity,
these traits are tempered by the fact that competition in the city
is keen. In other words, because of its size, many people are striving for the same freedom within the city. For example, there
tends to be a much greater demand for jobs than are available. So
while there is more freedom in the city than in rural areas, the
city dweller's freedom comes at a price. The price is seen in the
plight of the poor or homeless families who become the victims
of freedom.

Others see the city as the center of power, assimilation, and
diversity. Typically cities are centers of power and influence.
Rural areas have very little political and economic power primarily because government and bureaucratic offices are located
in downtown centers. Most jobs are located in and around the

cities, making them an economic power. The Chamber of Commerce, banks, and other financial institutions concentrate their offices in metropolitan areas. A good example of a city that functions as a center of power is the nation's capital, Washington, D.C. The surrounding suburban communities even as far away as Annapolis, Maryland, recognize that decisions made in Washington determine the amount of money they will receive for education, highway construction, and other things.

Assimilation, the process of merger and absorption, occurs in the city. The city has the unique quality of absorbing various groups within its boundaries in a dynamic life flow. Because of this, many ethnic groups are able to reside within its borders. This situation can be illustrated with a salad metaphor: The city is like a salad that has lettuce, tomatoes, peppers, onions, and carrots; when tossed, the salad absorbs all of its contents, yet the individual ingredients have not changed. Likewise, each culture in the city maintains its ethnic identity. Assimilation occurs because the social forces push people to identify with a particular ethnic group. Most groups maintain their identity but are absorbed into the dynamic flow of the city. When this phenomena occurs you may have a Hispanic brother or sister and an Asian brother or sister who live in different parts of Chicago and who have different cultures. But both say truly that they live in Chicago! Assimilation is where the rural area and the city are on common ground. In the country assimilation is as strong as in the city. There are certain modes of behavior, dress, and dialect that characterize people who live in the city and people who live in the country.

While the city is a place of power and assimilation, it is also a place of diversity. This is where the city and the rural area are, perhaps, most dissimilar. Rural areas are characterized by similarity. In the city, diversity often competes with assimilation; though people want to belong to a particular group, they also want to maintain some individuality or group distinction. For example, while ethnic groups like African-Americans, Hispanics, and Asians seek to maintain their own identity and diversity, some individuals seek to be distinct within that ethnic group.

Different people have different cultural behavior patterns. For example, in the city one can travel from block to block and experience Italian, German, Puerto Rican, or Thai art, food, and clothing. The splendor of diversity within the city is that virtually all countries of the world are represented in the U.S. Hence the city, unlike the rural areas, acts as a microcosm of the world. Roger S. Greenway observes, "People from all nations are coming to America. They crowd our cities. In short, the ends of the earth have come to town."[6] This shows that many cultures from other countries are now in the cities of America.

The city is also a place of change and transition. Because of the constant mobility of people moving in, out, and within the city, change is inevitable. Neighborhoods change over time as different ethnic groups transition in and out. This constant process of movement is what gives the city its dynamic nature. That dynamic nature makes the city a living organism that grows and is constantly in the process of change. Unlike the city, rural areas are not dynamic but static. Part of the freedom of the city is its mobility. Still, the reality of mobility must be tempered by the tendency of many ethnic groups to remain in a specific geographical locale. Some ethnic groups, for example, stay in the same neighborhoods for generations. This is partly because they choose to stay among "their own kind" and partly because racism and discrimination keep them there. Yet the city remains much more mobile than rural areas.

Many still view the city with disdain as a place of crime and alienation. It is perhaps this perception that most distinguishes rural communities from urban communities. Harvie Conn observed, "The image of the city for most white North Americans is negative."[7] The reality of crime in the city is indisputable, yet the negative view is out of proportion with reality. People don't talk about the rising rates of crime in rural areas. And in discussing crime, people tend to talk about violence, not "white collar" crimes such as embezzlement or misappropriation of funds. Also, whites fear blacks in the city, not recognizing that blacks being victimized by blacks is a much larger problem than whites being victimized by blacks. The reality is that crime is not a "city" problem. It is a problem wherever one goes. City folk are no more prone to crime than anyone else in the rest of society. Crime anywhere is the manifestation of humanity's universal rebellion against the laws of God.

Alienation is another characteristic of city life. As a result of crime, people are hesitant to trust strangers or even be neighborly. This produces a kind of alienation that many city folk experience. However, the same scenario can be said of the rural area as well. More and more people in rural areas are experiencing alienation.

City Life

To live in the city is to have one's senses stimulated. The frequent sounds of the police, emergency medical service, fire truck sirens, and the constant sounds of automobile horns are part of what it means to live in the city. City life also means seeing people live in drug-infested, dilapidated apartment houses. Ghettos are filled with anxiety, fear, poverty, and hopelessness. The smell of the ghettos is the scent of junkies looking for their next fix, abandoned buildings filled with trash, street corners filled with the homeless, or a drunk who is begging for a dollar. These kinds of sights, sounds, and smells can produce despair in people and break down their hope in the inner city. The tragedy of this, as Harv Oostdyk points out, is that

> ghetto doesn't consist of just winos and drug addicts and pimps and prostitutes and welfare cheats and thieves. Each block in the ghetto has strong reliable people, but these folks have been overcome by the rest.[8]

And then there is urbanization. David Claerbaut says, "Urbanization is an irreversible trend. In fact, about one-half of the world's population now lives in urban areas."[9] To experience urbanization is to observe the common characteristics of the urban context: size, ethnic, cultural, and religious diversity.

People flock to the city for various reasons: some for the conveniences the city offers, others for economic and business opportunities, and still others, to be near their work. All of these elements stimulate urbanization.

The result of the process of urbanization is often urban decline. Too many people living in the cities did not like the smell, sight, and sound of what was transpiring around them. The so-called suburban flight in the decades following World War II had a devastating effect upon cities. In the 1980s, major cities such as New York, Cleveland, and Baltimore were discussing dramatic cutbacks in city services and even possible bankruptcy. Claerbaut addresses these problems in saying,

> The process of urban deterioration follows a pattern. As the affluent move out, businesses head for suburban developments and malls. The absence of business and strong middle-class erodes the tax base so that, without government aid, cities head for bankruptcy.[10]

Moreover, the net effect of the suburban flight was the feminization of poverty, increased numbers of homelessness, and a rising epidemic of illegal drug users. Harvie Conn's analysis is insightful:

> Central city manufacturing was being drawn to the suburbs, attracted by local and federal tax breaks and the proximity of interstates and free-ways for easy access to transportation; industrial parks were popping up everywhere.... This move to a service-oriented economy divided the city into two cities—downtown and inner city.[11]

The downtown area was the place of city government and businesses, whereas the inner city was the place for the emerging residential underclass.

Finally, perception, myth, and stereotype often seem more real for some people than the actual reality. In discussing how the city functions in comparison with rural areas, myths and stereotypes rule the day. The city is seen as the place of horror and evil, while rural areas are glorified as the place of safety. The fact is, as Gulick stated, "There is a continuum between city and country."[12] One can find, for example, just as much homogeneity in the city, particularly in ethnic sections, as in the country. Also, in certain ethnic communities, traditions are preserved as steadfastly as they are in the country. Urban areas need to be perceived differently because, although the profane seems to be more visible, God is nevertheless raising up a prophetic church that will proclaim and reclaim the city as a sacred place.

Summary

In this chapter I have tried to provide the context of the city that is important for understanding the importance of urban church education. The suburban-rural model of ministry is very different from the urban model, but it still prevails where the urban model is needed. Finally, I have shown the effects of urbanization and described what living in the city is like.

Questions for Discussion

1. Explain what is meant by the term *urbanization*.
2. In making comparisons between urban, suburban, and rural life, does the author seem biased toward one or the other? Why or why not?
3. The author states that, on the one hand, the city has a way of absorbing or assimilating various ethnic groups, yet, on the other hand, "each culture maintains an ethnic identity." Do you think the author is contradicting himself? Why or why not?
4. In discussing how community development can empower the poor and the underclass, the author supports the idea of "community representation." What is its weakness? For example, how can the Christian character of the program be maintained if the community representatives are not Christians? Create a case-study scenario to discuss this point.

A Senior Adult Care and Enrichment Program

According to a 1990 published report by the American Association of Retired People (AARP), about 2.2 million Americans are 65 years old or older. The Adult Center for Enrichment, established in 1994 in Greensboro, North Carolina, is an adult daycare service. It provides daily respite care designed to meet the needs of older adults. The center, funded in part by the United Way, provides the technical support by training volunteers and provides the expertise for running the program at the local church level.

Two churches operate an adult respite program in conjunction with the Adult Center for Enrichment: First Baptist and Muirs Chapel United Methodist.

The general structure of the center's church-based program is that several days a week, older adults are dropped off at a church facility and picked up later in the day. The people are served breakfast and lunch during the course of the day. There are regularly scheduled activities such as library visits and trips to the local museums. The program provides health-care information. The respite program is specifically designed for older adults who are in fairly good health, although the center is able to provide services to those who are weak and frail.

Ann K. Umstead, executive director of the Adult Center for Enrichment, says that the church-based program is very adaptable to different settings. It can be organized to be a full-time adult daycare program operating five days a week, or it can be part-time, operating two or three days a week. The adaptability of the program depends on the facility and the needs of the community.

Churches like First Baptist or Muirs Chapel United Methodist provide the facilities. There is little cost to the church except for utilities and custodial care. The cost of the daycare program is $18.00 per hour per adult. Mrs. Umstead says she tries to connect with local churches because church-based programs tend to be reliable and successful.

"The church has an obligation to embrace the reality of the older adult population by empowering them to live the remainder of their lives in dignity," she says.[13]

Anita Brock Canter, the onsite program director at First Baptist and Muirs Chapel United Methodist churches, says the program is progressing strongly. The program at First Baptist provides adult daycare. It focuses on giving the participants a positive social interaction and a sense of independence. It started out very small—just two older adults—but grew to serve ten older adults. "The elderly in our community were resistant to going to agencies for help or assistance, but they would come to churches. So the program was birthed out of the need to help the elderly and to get local churches involved," Mrs. Carter said.[14]

First Baptist's downtown location and the individual attention participants receive from the staff have contributed to its success. The program meets three times a week. The participants plan the activities for each day in advance, including reading the newspaper, light exercise, and games. Mrs. Carter said the program is prepared to respond to the challenges that come with working with the elderly. For example, some participants have shown signs of emerging Alzheimer's disease, and the staff is trained to work with such people.

According to a 1996 brochure, the Adult Center for Enrichment has the following goals: "to provide adult day care/day health for employed caregivers to relieve stress of the need for daily supervision of an adult family member who cannot stay by themselves" and "to provide improved quality of life for the adult family member . . . through maintenance of peer relationships and friendships and opportunities for successful daily experiences."[15] Mrs. Carter believes the program is achieving its goals. These goals are witnessed by how much the participants enjoy the program and have taken ownership of it. The participants enjoy connecting with each other, the predictability of the program, and the independence it gives them.

In most major metropolitan areas there are various agencies like the Adult Center for Enrichment that can team up with churches for this kind of program.

The agency provides the expertise while the church provides the participants and the facility.

For additional information, contact Mrs. Ann K. Umstead or Mrs. Anita B. Carter at the Adult Center for Enrichment, 301 Washington Square, Suite 111, Greensboro, NC 27401, or call (336) 274–3359.

CHAPTER 4

Liberated to Learn

Principles of Empowering Education

The heart and soul of urban church education is empowerment and transformation. The poor and the oppressed do not need theories about their condition. What they need is empowerment that will equip them to transform their situation. Urban church education seeks to bring together empowerment, equipping, and transformation. Ecclesiastes 4:12 says, "A threefold cord is not quickly broken." I believe the underclass, those who live in ghettos, can be empowered and equipped through the local church to transform their wastelands into beautiful gardens.[1] This must not be understood as utopian idealism. The idea of transforming ghettos into gardens is a dream that should motivate everyone who is concerned about the city—a dream that is embedded in the reality that the local church, adopting an empowerment approach to education, can make a significant difference in the inner city.

Education as liberation is the theme that brings this book together. This liberation is freedom from ignorance, poverty, welfare dependence, and low self-worth. It is a spiritual freedom that comes as a result of being empowered and leads to transformation. An empowerment approach avoids the problem of "narration sickness," according to Paulo Freire.[2] Traditionally educators,

Freire says, understood their role as lecturers to students, depositing bits of information into their minds, similar to a person depositing money into a bank account. The student is essentially an empty receptor waiting to be filled by the teacher. "This is the banking concept of education,"[3] which Freire views as shortchanging a student of serious inquiry and a desire to learn.

What this means for urban church education is simply that students will not be empowered to transform their situation by using the "banking concept" Freire criticizes. On the contrary, students must be able to practically engage the knowledge they are receiving. Such knowledge must be relevant, contextual, and user friendly. An empowering approach seeks to equip students with the knowledge they need to transform their situation in life. In addition, it boosts self-confidence, energizes self-reliance, and ignites self-motivation to achieve planned goals.

The Need for Empowerment

There are several nuances to the meaning of the word *empower*. It may be defined from a judicial-legal perspective as "the right to invest with legal power," such as when someone is given the power of attorney. To have the power of attorney means that one can execute a will or sign legal documents on behalf of someone else. Another nuance, related to the first, is "to authorize." That is, one gives authority to another to perform some duty or task. Moreover, to authorize carries with it the connotation of the right or legitimacy to act or perform some duty. Still another nuance is "to enable or permit." Again, this is similar to the first, yet this nuance gets to the heart of the matter. To enable means to make capable, to equip someone to do or to perform a task that otherwise could not be accomplished. To enable is to provide someone with the skills, knowledge, and information necessary to function as and be an achiever. Biblically, God is the one who empowers people to accomplish his will. The prefix *em-* means to give power to someone who did not have it before.

Biblical examples of empowerment illustrate this definition. In Judges 3:10, "the spirit ["Spirit," NKJV] of the LORD"
came upon Othniel and empowered him to deliver the
Israelites from the hand of Cushan-Rishathaim, the king of
Mesopotamia. In Judges 11:29, "the spirit of the LORD" empowered Jephthah to gain victory over the Ammonites. And in
Judges 13:25, "the spirit of the LORD" came upon Samson and
empowered him to perform extraordinary deeds of physical
strength. With each of these men, power was "put into" them
by the Holy Spirit. This empowerment was not natural to these
biblical characters but was given to them by God to achieve
and to accomplish his will.

In similar manner to the old covenant examples in Judges,
the new covenant believer is also to be empowered to achieve
God's purposes. In Luke 24:49 Jesus mentions that the disciples
were waiting for the "promise" of the Father to be fulfilled in
them when they were "endued with power from on high."
According to *Strong's Concordance*, the Greek word translated as
"endued" means "to be clothed with." It is used to create the
metaphor of someone putting on a garment. Jesus is essentially
telling his disciples that they must be empowered before they
can accomplish God's will. This empowerment would come
from "on high" in the person of the Holy Spirit.

In his second volume—the book of Acts—Luke continues
this same line of thought. He records Jesus' teaching the disciples that they will receive power when the Holy Spirit comes
upon them (Acts 1:8). The *Spirit Filled Life Bible* points out that
"the distinctive purpose of the outpouring of the Spirit in Acts is
to empower the church for ministry."[4]

✳ The classic Pentecostal movement has been particularly
motivated in seeking to experience the power of the Holy Spirit.
If the disciples needed to be empowered by the Holy Spirit for
ministry and witness, then so does the believer today. The
church of Jesus Christ must rediscover the reality and the
empowering presence of the Holy Spirit.

From Liberation to Empowerment

Many in the Third World embrace the theology of liberation, which came out of a Latin American context, as a theological motif that accurately articulates their situation. In the Third World, poverty, injustice, and oppression are commonplace. Gustavo Gutiérrez argues that the Word of God must effect change by liberating the poor and the oppressed in this environment.[5] In the United States a "black theology of liberation" reflects upon the brutal, historical reality of slavery and oppression for black people. This theology articulates what was happening politically in the civil rights movement of the mid-1960s.[6]

J. Deotis Roberts disagrees with Cone's identification of black theology with the radical black power movement. He argues instead that black theology is not only liberation, but also reconciliation. For Cone, black theology separates the races, but for Roberts it reconciles them in Christ.[7] Although these men have a different emphasis in their theology, they both root it in the idea of liberation. Blacks need liberation from the oppression and injustice that exists in the United States.

My purpose here is to propose that a new theological motif of empowerment must arise. If black people are politically liberated but are spiritually in shackles to sin and a poverty mentality, can this be called liberation? How has liberation benefited the staggering number of black people who are called the "underclass" by sociologists? What about the phenomenon of the ungodly number of young black males who are murdered every year in our urban centers?

Political liberation and the civil rights movement were indeed necessary. But the current social and political climate demands a new theological base to address the problems that continue to affect the urban poor. King Zedekiah asked the prophet Jeremiah a poignant question: "Is there any word from the LORD?" Jeremiah said unequivocally, "There is" (Jeremiah 37:17). This is the same question that the underclass is asking the church today. I believe that the word from the Lord today is simply "empowerment." The practical problem associated with achieving some measure of political liberation is that it can lead to an individualistic, "do your own thing" mentality. This is all too similar to the unfaithful Israelites in the Old Testament. Judges 21:25 says, "In those days there was no king in Israel; everyone did that which was right in his own eyes." Instead, consider this point made by Carl Ellis:

> True liberation is not the right to do what I want, it is the power to do what is right. If we are going to achieve the liberation of our historical quest, then we must go beyond liberation to righteousness—God's righteousness.[8]

In our natural strength we cannot achieve the righteousness of God, but with God's empowerment we can.

Principles of Empowering Education

In chapter 1 I defined urban church education and said that it seeks to empower people to function as and to be achievers. Only through achievement can a positive self-image be cultivated. In attempting to empower people who live in the inner city, one will inevitably encounter what William H. Cook refers to as the "failure image."[9] The failure image is the concept individuals have about themselves in light of the realities of their lives. Basically, the failure image is produced by low self-esteem and a lack of goals. The problem is that the daily reality of life has a way of wearing down self-ambition. Therefore, from a psychological perspective, one principle of empowerment is *the development of a positive self-image.* Empowerment must emphasize the biblical principles that humankind is created in the image of God (Genesis 1:27). As a creation of God, each person has a unique gift and calling that God knows. The real challenge in life, therefore, is to discover the reason why we were created and then fulfill that purpose.

An empowering educational principle related to this is *boosting self-esteem and motivating a person to achieve with confidence.* Self-esteem is enhanced when students, having learned that they are "somebody" because they are creations of God, are repeatedly affirmed with encouraging words and warm support. But this is not enough. A person can continue to have a poor self-concept even when receiving affirmation. A second step is necessary: The achievement of a specific goal. Only when a person achieves a predetermined goal joined with encouraging words will self-esteem be strongly attained. Hence, the more success a person achieves, the stronger the self-esteem will be. By "success" I mean "the progressive realization of a person's worthwhile, predetermined goals."[10] People who are truly empowered are those who recognize their self-worth as a creation of God and are motivated to achieve worthwhile, predetermined goals.

Another principle in empowering education is that *every situation has a specific context.* By "context" I mean that the neighborhood is examined in its entirety. The urban situation must not be approached with the mentality that one size fits all. For example, even though a food pantry works in one neighborhood, it may not meet the need in another; perhaps somewhere else some day-care service for single mothers is a greater need. Or, suppose that in a particular neighborhood there are large numbers of boys and girls "hanging around" street corners near a local church. The children leave school several hours before their parents arrive home from work. The local church could establish a program of after-school care to provide the boys and girls with a safe, positive place to go during that interim. In addition, the after-school program can offer help with homework and provide mentors for the children. This is an example of using the empowering educational principle of context.

Moreover, the empowering educational principle of context emphasizes *an incarnational identity with the neighborhood.* When a church has properly "read" the community and is sensitive to its particular needs, it takes upon itself a unique identity there. Such an identity will cause the neighborhood to view not only the empowering educational program, but also the church as theirs. When the community claims the church as its own, the church truly becomes God's instrument to empower.

It is also a principle of empowering education to *place equal stress on orthopraxis and orthodoxy*. "Orthopraxis" means correct practice, while "orthodoxy" means correct belief. Ideally, there should be no discrepancy between what a person believes and what a person does. But in the real world, discrepancies exist; there are doctrines without actions, words without deeds. Biblical empowerment comes from the constant interaction between action and reflection, action leading to reflection, and reflection leading again to action in a continual process of correction and amplification of both elements.

The local church is essential for putting empowering educational principles into practice. The vision of this book is to see the local church become what Jesus metaphorically described in Matthew 5:14 as a city "set on a hill." I believe the local church can once again rise above the common stereotype that it lacks authority and can reclaim its rightful place at the center of the community. If the local church in an urban context embraces empowering educational principles, it can reestablish its ministry in the community. Then the Lord might once again anoint the church for special service. Then also, the church can proclaim the spiritual truths of the gospel with more integrity and credibility. The major hindrance to becoming a city set on a hill is not rival religious institutions like the Nation of Islam or Jehovah's Witnesses, but the division and isolation among the leaders and denominations of the church. I think that Francis Frangipane is correct when he says, "Our cities are in disorder because the church is in disorder."[11]

To adequately address the demons of poverty, oppression, and injustice, the church needs to unite itself around empowering educational principles. Frangipane is very insightful when he comments,

> It will take a citywide church to win the citywide war. Our separate isolated efforts will not stop the flood of increasing evil in our cities if we, as Christ's church, remain isolated from each other.[12]

Summary

In this chapter I establish a definition of empowerment that urban church educators can use as a guide. Empowerment means being enabled or equipped to achieve some goal. Although liberation is a crucial theological theme for those who are poor and oppressed, it is incomplete without empowerment. Liberation certainly frees the oppressed or the poor, but empowerment equips them to move toward achieving goals.

I also explain various principles of empowering education. Finally, I offer a vision of the urban church reestablishing credibility within its neighborhood.

Questions for Discussion

1. Do you agree or disagree with the author's view that education is equal to liberation and empowerment? Why or why not?
2. In *Pedagogy of the Oppressed*, Paulo Freire talks about "narration sickness." What do you think he means by this term? Is the author justified in using this language?
4. The author contends that urban church education must move beyond liberation as a basic theological motif to empowerment. How does he support this view? What are the strengths and weaknesses of this position?

A G.E.D. Program

Myrtle Lawson is a retired elementary school teacher and one of the leaders of the General Equivalence Diploma (G.E.D.) program at Cana Baptist Church in Washington, D.C. "How strange it is that the Lord placed me in elementary education for over twenty-five years and now, retired, I am working with adults," Mrs. Lawson says.[13] Cana Baptist Church is an African-American congregation that was established in 1947 with a mission to help the poor and needy in its community. The G.E.D. program, begun in October 1996, is part of this mission.

The initial vision of the program was a community learning center that would include computer training classes. About a year later, organizers decided that participants really needed help with remedial skills in reading, writing, and math. The program seeks to prepare students to take the G.E.D. exam so that they can get better jobs. "Without the appropriate skills the students will continue to remain on the welfare rolls," says Mrs. Lawson.

The curriculum is a standard G.E.D. preparatory manual available in bookstores, and the courses meet the requirements for preparing students to take the G.E.D. examination. Attendance varies from six to eight students, with ages ranging from seventeen to sixty. To accommodate various schedules, classes are held on weekday evenings and during the day on Saturdays. To participate, students complete a simple registration form and are interviewed to measure their needs. The teachers are members of the church and teach on a volunteer basis. This means the program can be offered at no cost to the students. The program is advertised by word of mouth and flyers distributed in the community.

The program has been successful in that a number of students have obtained their G.E.D. and go on to better jobs. And these students credit the Cana Baptist program for their achievement.

Several factors lie behind the success of the program. First, the instructors are all former teachers who volunteer their time because they recognize the importance of a solid education. Second, the class sizes are very small, which allows for one-on-one instruction. Third, the course schedule is flexible and sensitive to students' needs. For example, Mrs. Lawson was scheduled to meet with her students in a reading class in the early evening, but because a few students suggested a morning time, she moved the class time.

One challenge for the program is that the community surrounding Cana Baptist Church is predominantly Latino. The church is looking for ways to expand the G.E.D. program into that community. One obstacle could be a shortage of volunteer teachers who know Spanish. Another is the lack of an effective means of communicating information to the community.

Among African-Americans, however, inquiries continue to increase and the program continues to grow. Others in the community see the program as filling a great need. Sandra Butler Truesdale, who works for the District of Columbia school board, said, "The program at Cana Baptist Church is one of the few G.E.D. programs sponsored by a local church in the city."

Mrs. Myrtle Lawson can be contacted at Cana Baptist Church, 1607 Monroe Street, N.W. Washington, D.C. 20007, or (202) 234–5330.

CHAPTER 5

In Order to Succeed

Constructing a Christian Education Ministry

Evangel Temple is a mega-church in the inner city of Washington, D.C. It was started in the mid-1950s by Reverend John L. Meares, who was ordained by the Church of God (Cleveland, Tennessee). One of the unique features about Evangel Temple is that although the founding pastor is a white man, the congregation is African-American. Over the years the church has survived many battles both externally and internally and stands today as a remarkable testament to one man's faith in the God who called him to the city. Pastor Meares has always preached a message of hope and empowerment. For most of the church's history the congregation was composed of poor working-class blacks, and John Meares had the ability to inspire and empower them to reach beyond racism and prejudice toward God.

Today the church continues to be a successful church filled with working-to-upper-class families. Their facilities are currently located outside the city in the predominantly black County of Prince George, Maryland. I was brought on staff in March 1983 to direct the growing Christian education ministry and to develop a lay training Bible school.[1] The Bible school and educational program were built on an empowering model. In other words, Pastor Meares wanted to move beyond preaching to and saving souls. He was adamant that Evangel Temple must be about saving lives. This was achieved through a variety of programs to families, senior citizens, and the poor. Therefore, the focus of the Christian education ministry and the Bible school was to equip and to empower people to change their lives—their lifestyles and life situations.

As I reflect upon my time at Evangel Temple, I realize that our program was successful in two ways. First, it transformed people's spiritual lives. Second, it had a lot of support. It was one of the few churches in Washington that had a full-time, salaried staff person leading its education ministry. It had an abundance of volunteer workers and a variety of programs for each age group. From the late 1970s to the mid-1980s, dozens of churches attended workshops and seminars sponsored by Evangel Temple's Christian education ministry. At that time, few independent Pentecostal churches had given much attention to this topic; now, more churches have solid Christian education ministries.

The Call to Teach

In 1967, Pastor Meares sensed the Lord telling him that He desired His people to be settled and grounded in the Bible. This instruction stressed the necessity of teaching God's flock the biblical basis for their faith. Just as our physical bodies need food for energy and growth, so spiritual food is necessary for the life and growth of our spiritual nature.

Through Pastor Meares's instruction in God's Word, the church discovered that being "born again" is a tremendous experience but is just the beginning of new life in Jesus Christ. The Christian is saved to be a servant in God's kingdom. Furthermore, the church came to realize that after the born-again experience the believer must be discipled and taught basic principles to become strong and knowledgeable. With this emphasis, believers are empowered to do God's will and achieve success in life.

In the late 1960s and early 1970s, Evangel Temple began to conduct instructional courses such as the very popular nine-month catechism class. This was an elementary course that taught believers the basics of the Christian faith and practice. The distinctiveness of these courses started attracting people from all over the city. It was not unusual for the classes at Evangel Temple to have 200 to 500 students.

Before it became successful, however, the church had to ask some serious questions:

1. *Do We Really Desire a Teaching Ministry?* This may seem an unnecessary question to ask. Yet, the point not to be overlooked here is that there is a cost involved in making a local church a teaching force for God.

2. *What Are Some of the Resources Needed for a Teaching Ministry?* The answers to this question can be overwhelming, but they do not have to stop us in our tracks. We can become so bogged down in issues such as curriculum needs, qualifications of teachers, evaluation procedures, and facility constraints that we lose sight of this fact: We need to start where we are and use what we have.

3. *How Do We Solve the Problems of Teacher Commitment and Discipline?* In most urban churches these are perplexing issues. Given the general decline of attendance in Sunday school overall, the question of commitment is problematic. However, this doesn't need to deter us; we can step out in faith. At Evangel Temple we developed a solid teacher-training program that involved classes on how to teach. We also emphasized team teaching and mentoring. Commitment and discipline increased as prospective teachers were exposed to our rigorous training program. It became the goal of the teacher-training instructors to provide the excellence of ministry that the Lord requires.

Foundational Principles

Jesus said "Go therefore and make disciples ... , teaching them to observe all things that I have commanded you" (Matthew 28:19–20 NKJV).

The purpose of the education ministry at Evangel Temple comes in response to that Great Commission. The planning and implementation of a Christian education ministry must support and reinforce this commandment. To follow His commandment, however, Evangel Temple had to search for ways to make biblical mandates meaningful to prospective teachers. That process meant breaking down Jesus' commandment into bite-sized pieces so that it could be digested and communicated to these people. Also, we had to keep in mind that we were working with volunteers.

It is important here to make the distinction between a casual learner and a disciple. Disciples are learners who are willing to make earnest attempts to change their lifestyle and behavior patterns in accordance with what is being taught. In fact, the Greek word *mathetes* means one who is committed to the teaching of another and is therefore a learner. The difference is that learners may be willing to gather all the information they can, but may make no earnest attempts to take responsibility for what they learn. The key to making disciples is to teach and train.

By definition, teachers are responsible to train and instruct. This instruction takes place with the understanding that—

1. We are "doing" the creative acts of God (not our own things).
2. The potential disciples are learners who are willing to make earnest attempts to change their lifestyle.

With these expectations, it becomes the teacher's responsibility to learn to teach in a way that will facilitate the student's ability to learn. All teachers in the Evangel Temple education ministry must be willing to undergo the training necessary to enhance their skills.

The writer of Hebrews 5:11–14 points out that those who have never mastered the fundamentals cannot really grasp more advanced truths and that until they have been fed milk, they cannot handle the meat of the Word. With this in mind, the church began to teach the foundational principles found in Hebrews 6:1–3.

Through these six principles, believers become mature in their Christian walk. When Evangel Temple began teaching these principles, many members became more committed to God and the church began to grow numerically.

We also taught the principles of covenant relationships: God's relationship to mankind, and mankind's relationship to one another through the Holy Spirit. The essence of covenant is that two become one: "And the glory which You gave Me I have given them, that they may be one just as We are one" (John 17:22 NKJV). When people become believers, they become one with the Lord as He is one with the Father. The God who undertook to save undertakes also to live His life in them.

As the people were being fed these basic foundational scriptural principles, a wonderful miracle was taking place. People began hungering and thirsting for spiritual reality and consequently grew in their maturity in Christ. As the people's spiritual needs were met, they began inviting others to attend. In the mid-1970s, Evangel Temple had about three hundred people in attendance, mostly women. But as the church remained obedient to God's Word to feed His people, it witnessed a steady, consistent growth in numbers. Whole families were being drawn to the church. Soon the adult congregation grew from 20 percent males and 80 percent females to approximately 45 percent males and 55 percent females!

The Teacher Training Program: An Overview

"Study to show thyself approved unto God, a workman that needeth not to be ashamed, rightly dividing the word of truth" (2 Timothy 2:15).

With the church growing both numerically and spiritually, Evangel Temple felt the need to draft a plan for the teaching ministry that included a purpose statement with goals and objectives. The strategy was finalized into an action plan that looked like this:

I.   Purpose:

    A. To provide all students with consistent and systematic teaching that will lead to a clear understanding of the principles that govern how to live an empowered life in Jesus Christ.

    B. To provide adult staff with teaching and training that will increase their knowledge of the teaching/learning process.

II.   Goals:

    A. To maintain a unified, comprehensive, and balanced curriculum.

    B. To empower students and to become actively, consistently committed to studying God's Word.

    C. To build and maintain qualified leadership able to effectively empower others for leadership.

III. Action Plans:

The action plans (strategies) are teacher training and leadership programs that consist of the following components.

    A. Teach with Confidence

        Primary course for teacher training; Bible-centered ministry; team teaching; teacher/leader training, staff meetings, quarterly workshops, and annual retreats.

        "And He Himself gave some to be apostles, some prophets, some evangelists, and some pastors and teachers, for the equipping of the saints for the work of ministry" (Ephesians 4:11–12 NKJV).

    B. Equipping the Saints

        Equipping the saints to stir up the gifts that are within them is a major part of the church's responsibility.

Also, it is the church's responsibility to help prospective teachers realize that the gift to teach is from the Lord and that this gift operates by the power of the Holy Spirit. Another aspect of the church's responsibility is to train volunteers so that they understand what is expected of them as teachers. This is done by helping them realize that while they receive help from the Holy Spirit, it is their responsibility to (1) understand the Word of God as it relates to the subject to be taught; and (2) prepare their lessons empowered by the Holy Spirit who works through them.

With this in mind, we now ask, what are the practical components for teaching?

I. Teacher Training Course

Teach with Confidence is a foundational thirteen-week course developed by the Evangelical Teaching Association and designed for teacher training. It is offered twice a year, in the fall and in the spring. One major objective of the course is to impart an in-depth understanding of the teaching/learning process for prospective teachers. In this class prospective teachers learn that effective teaching and learning occur in orderly, cyclical steps. Further, they learn that one must be sensitive and teach according to the ways pupils learn. As a result, prospective teachers are taught that the learning cycle has five phases:

A. Approach—identify the need. Go from the known to the unknown

B. Explore—search for the truth in Scripture

C. Discover—find the answer to fit the need

D. Appropriate—relate the truth to life and need

E. Assume responsibility—change in lifestyle

The learning cycle will be explained in further detail in the next chapter.

Most importantly, prospective teachers come to understand that empowering education seeks a change in behavior of the student that leads to spiritual maturity. Thus the teacher's role is a vital one, because he or she can lead the student to the fountain of biblical insights—but the learner must take a drink.

II. The Lesson Plan

Another important goal is to teach participants the importance of a lesson plan and how to use it. A lesson plan outlines a specific plan of action for one day's lesson and encompasses the use of the teaching/learning cycle. It is a step-by-step arrangement of information, materials, and methods a teacher uses to help the pupil learn. It is a tool that helps the teacher organize time spent with the student. The lesson plan helps the teacher use every minute as efficiently as possible. I know from experience that it is challenging to convince Sunday school teachers of the value and importance of preparing lesson plans. But promoting this discipline among your teachers is worth the effort, especially when they notice how focused and organized their lessons are because of lesson plans. The lesson plan consists of the following parts:

A. The aim of the lesson: What is the purpose of the lesson?

B. The goals of the lesson: What are the steps toward achieving the lesson?

C. Objectives of the lesson: To what purpose or goal are you teaching?

D. Methods to be used:
   1. Visual aids and materials
   2. Scriptural reference and memory verse
   3. Bible exploration (Find out what truth you want discovered.)
   4. Bible application (How does this truth relate to the student's life?)
   5. Decision (Going on to maturity)

E. Assuming responsibility—Helping the students see how this applies to their life personally.

III. Lesson Evaluation

Evaluation is measuring the extent to which teachers have achieved their lesson aim. Evaluation helps teachers measure the effectiveness of the lesson and assists them in making improvements. Before useful lesson evaluations can occur, teachers must have written standards by which to measure their classroom presentation. The following are examples of questions prospective teachers learn to ask in evaluating their lessons:

A. Did I make the aim clear to the students?

B. Did the beginning of the lesson catch the attention of the pupils?

C. Was the opening approach the best I could use?

D. Was each point clearly understood by all?

E. Did I involve the students in the lesson?

F. Do I feel the Lord was pleased with the way I presented His Holy Word?

G. Did the pupils understand how the teaching applied to their lives?

These sample evaluation questions are yardsticks to measure teaching excellence. All the students who complete *Teach with Confidence* and make a decision to join the teaching staff are given assistance in defining their role as a teacher. Furthermore, this course is structured to allow maximum input and participation from class members. Lectures on topics are followed by the presentation of a lesson based on the previous week's discussion. Teachers share their lesson plans with class members. The ultimate goal is to train participants to adapt the content and teaching methods presented in class into lesson plans for specific age groups.

IV. Team Teaching

The team-teaching approach is used in the classroom with children, teens, and young adults. In team teaching, participants learn more as they put what they have learned into practice. Observing the techniques of other members of the teaching team serves as on-the-job training and as a way to enhance teaching skills. This apprenticeship model has proved successful as less experienced teachers work with more experienced ones; this builds confidence. The course lessons, planned in series, embrace all aspects of the teaching/learning cycle, using a multimedia technique to enhance the lessons. It is important that teachers learn to apply the practical methods covered in this course to every age group.

V. Bible-Centered Ministry

The key to a successful teaching ministry is a focus on the Bible. Second Timothy 3:14–16 tells us that the Scriptures make one wise for salvation through faith in Christ Jesus: "All Scripture is given by inspiration of God, and is profitable for doctrine, for reproof, for correction, for instruction in righteousness, that the man of God may be complete, thoroughly equipped for every good work" (v. 16 NKJV).

James 1:22 says, "But be doers of the word, and not hearers only, deceiving yourselves" (NKJV). The purpose of Bible study is to empower and change lives. Therefore the desired outcome of the Bible teaching ministry of your church should be a progressive, positive change in the life of each learner—a change that leads to spiritual maturity. A changed life is one empowered to be an achiever in life. Thus a key component in a teacher training program is "Bible-centered ministry," to which prospective teachers are taught to apply the following criteria for teaching God's Word:

A. Curriculum Development: What types of courses should be taught and in what sequence?

B. Biblical Evangelism: Does the lesson have room for evangelism?

C. Learner-Centered Focus: Is the lesson taught in such a way that students can learn? Or is it focused upon the teacher?

D. Learner involvement: How much participation do students have in the lesson?

E. The Learning Process: How do students grasp what is taught?

F. The Teacher's Role: Does the teacher guide, inform, monitor, and model the classroom?

VI. *Teacher/Learner Training*

"... But, speaking the truth in love, may grow up in all things into Him, who is the head—Christ" (Ephesians 4:15 NKJV).

A. Discipline

As participants begin this initial training process, it soon becomes apparent that there is a need to exercise discipline in what they have learned. Through team teaching, teachers learn not to be a "weak link." It is through team interaction and evaluation that conscientious effort is made to be consistent in commitment to both Christian education and the local church.

B. Commitment

It is difficult to drop out of a team when you know that student teammates are counting on you. The commitment to the team is reinforced as team members encourage and edify one another and confess shortcomings to one another, all the while committed to one another to improve oneself.

C. Leadership Development

To further develop the teaching skills of those who want to be teachers, we required that they attend education ministry workshops, staff meetings, and retreats.

D. Workshops

Quarterly workshops are held to meet the demand for ongoing training and inspire the spirit of excellence in ministry. During the workshops a review of current techniques is used in teaching the students of all ages. Also, the workshops serve as opportunities for fellowship and sharing.

E. Staff Meetings

Staff meetings are held once a month and are required for teachers. At these meetings the teaching team has an opportunity to review personal problems or difficulties about specific children, then discuss how to solve these problems. Goals and objectives are reviewed and evaluated, adjustments being made as necessary. This is also a time for sharing new ideas and sharing information about such things as materials, parents, and children.

F. Retreats

This is a special time away from the familiar environment when teachers can be refreshed and revitalized as they listen to speakers who share teaching or ministry perspectives with them.

Summary

Like any church located in the city, Evangel Temple in Washington, D.C., wrestled with the direction of our Christian education program. This chapter has provided an approach to constructing an education ministry that captures the vision of urban Christian education. Also, I attempted to provide an overview of the training programs for teachers and some of the preliminary concerns to be addressed.

Questions for Discussion

1. Discuss some of the preliminary questions Evangel Temple had to address in constructing its education program.
2. How important is the Great Commission in Matthew 28:18–19 in constructing a Christian education ministry?
3. Review the teacher-training program and evaluate its strengths and weaknesses.
4. What will make the training program work in your specific context?
5. How is this chapter helpful in providing guidelines for constructing your Christian education ministry?

The Partners in Christ Mentoring Program

Mount Zion Baptist Church, one of the largest African-American churches in Greensboro, North Carolina, started a Partners in Christ (PIC) program in December 1994.[2] The program was founded, according to the Reverend Kevin Lee, then youth pastor and program coordinator, "for the expressed purpose of meeting the needs of young African-American males within the Mount Zion Church family. The program sought to assist single mothers who wanted a significant adult male presence in the lives of their sons."[3] In addition, the program is structured with a coordinating team that helps encourage the young men towards achievement.

The program is based on mentors. Lee said, "All mentors must be members in good standing at Mount Zion." An application process that involves an interview and police records check screens the mentors. According to a handout given to all mentors, youths, and parents, the program requires mentors to do the following:

1. Attend designated training sessions.
2. Encourage assigned youth to attend weekly Bible study.
3. Spend a minimum of two hours a month in face-to-face activities with their assigned youth.
4. Visit the youth at school a minimum of once every six weeks.
5. Contact the youth at least once a week.
6. Establish contact with parent(s) at least twice a month.

The program started with thirteen African-American boys around middle-school age. The program is not designed to handle any more than fifteen "because we want to maximize the individual attention each boy receives," Lee says. Some participants stay longer than others. The parents and the boys have the opportunity to evaluate the program and, overall, their evaluation is favorable. The boys enjoy doing activities with the mentor, and single mothers appreciate having the positive male role models for their sons.

I became aware of PIC through a parent whose son attended the Christian school where I served as the principal. The thirteen-year-old, whom we will call Darrell, was enrolled in PIC by his mother, who was single, because she felt he was getting involved with the wrong crowd at school and was not motivated to perform at the level of his academic potential. Speaking some eight months after her son entered the program, she said she observed some attitude changes in Darrell and saw the positive effect of his having a good male role model in his life. She says, "Darrell is still not too motivated regarding academics, but he enjoys sports and is a bit more interested in going to the young adult programs at Mount Zion. I am really grateful for that." Darrell expressed his appreciation for the program as only a thirteen-year-old boy can, saying that it was "all right." He did not mind interacting with his mentor, whom he described as "a nice man who enjoys sports and movies."

The benefits of this program are that it is not difficult to operate, yet has tremendous potential to address a serious problem and obvious need in the African-American community. This model, which focuses on boys who live with a single mother, can be replicated at other local churches. Unlike the Mount Zion program, it could include young people from outside the church. Also, I prefer a more specific and measurable mission statement than Mount Zion's, which states its focus as "the spiritual well-being of our youth."

For additional information, contact the Reverend Kevin Lee, Mount Zion Baptist Church, 1301 Alamance Church Road, Greensboro, NC 27406, or (910) 273–7930.

CHAPTER 6

Follow the Leader

Becoming an Empowering Teacher

I have learned that although many urban church educators are not trained in any method of education, they will use one, even if it is simply trial and error. So this chapter offers introductory information about basic educational methods. We can best learn to be effective teachers by studying the Master Teacher: the Lord Jesus Christ.

Jesus used effective methods in his teaching ministry that should be our guide. The Gospels provide us with just such a record from four different viewpoints. Moreover, Jesus is the Word, and it is through the Word that our lives are changed and empowered. Jesus is the Christian teacher's example and inspiration.

Someone once said that Jesus was often a healer, sometimes a worker of miracles, frequently a preacher, but always a teacher. Jesus used teaching as a primary means of conveying His message. He came into the world to share a life-changing message.

Jesus also perfectly embodied what He taught. He was "the way, the truth, and the life" (John 14:6). He understood His disciples inside and out and knew what they needed. At the end of His earthly ministry, Jesus gave his followers a teaching commission as the means of continuing what He had begun:

"Go therefore and make disciples of all the nations, baptizing them in the name of the Father and of the Son and of the Holy Spirit, teaching them to observe all things that I have commanded you" (Matthew 28:19–20 NKJV).

By saying this, Jesus Christ recognized teaching as essential to the building of the kingdom and Christian character.

Characteristics of Jesus' Teaching

Observe the following characteristics of the teaching ministry of Christ.

1. Jesus' Teaching Had Purpose

Jesus' purpose was the communication of revealed truth. He recognized His call and referred to Himself as one whose teachings were not self-initiated; He had been given a ministry by His Father (John 5:19, 30). There was no hesitancy, fear, or drawing back from the responsibilities that were His as a teacher sent by God. The power He possessed He put into His authoritative message. He taught with purpose. He never taught haphazardly, but with a clear goal and objective in mind, that of revealing the will of His Father.

2. Jesus' Teaching Had Distinctive Character

The New Testament tells us that Jesus taught with authority (Matthew 7:28–29). On one occasion the officers sent out by the chief priests to take Him prisoner came back with the report, "No man ever spoke like this Man!" (John 7:46 NKJV). He spoke as the representative of God.

Jesus taught creatively. One characteristic of His teachings that startled the Jewish rabbis was His departure from the traditional system of synagogue lectures. The Lord used almost every imaginable type of teaching technique to deliver His message of truth. He maintained the interest of His audience by using parables from everyday life. He made his message clear by using ordinary examples such as coins, seed, and sheep. Often he simply asked poignant questions of His audience.

3. Jesus' Teaching Had Discernible Results

Jesus' ministry resulted in changed lives. Study carefully the call of the disciples as recorded in Mark 1:16–39. Here is a vivid picture of Jesus teaching people and transforming them into disciples.

- Verse 16—Jesus *sought* them. They were ordinary men doing mundane things; He went where they were in order to change their lives.
- Verse 17—Jesus *called* them. He wasn't content to let them stand off on the sidelines. He deliberately commanded their attention by saying, "Follow me and I will make you fishers of men."
- Verse 21—Jesus *taught* them. For three years they were at His side observing His miracles, listening to His teachings, and accepting His personal counsel.
- Verse 34—Jesus *showed* them. His demonstration of power was to be a pattern for their ministry. The power of a teacher to heal the disease of ignorance and cast out the demon of apathy shouldn't be underestimated!
- Verses 38–39—Jesus *sent* them. While Jesus was still on earth, He constantly used His disciples in ministry to others. Christian education ministry is not an end in itself; it is a means to enhance the growth of Christians and the development of workers to accomplish the work of Christ.

Therefore, Christian teaching is the communication of Christ, the living Word, from the written word of the Bible through the spoken word of the teacher. The "gift" of teaching and the "call" of teaching are essential to effectively impart the Word of God. The gift and the call, however, will be most effective through training and thorough preparation. Nicodemus recognized Jesus as an exceptional teacher sent from God because of His miracles. In short, he witnessed results from Jesus' teaching.

4. Jesus' Strategy for Teaching

We do well to study the strategies Jesus used to fulfill His teaching ministry. The components of His ministry are as follows:

A. Evangelism
   1. Proactive ministry: "Go, ... serve to the masses" (and multitudes followed Him).
   2. A call to obedience: "Baptize all who believe."
   3. Recruitment: Jesus chose twelve men (His disciples).
   4. Jesus called them: "Come, follow Me." This challenge demanded a response.

B. Discipleship

As Jesus ministered to the masses, baptized believers, and recruited disciples, He transformed people's lives. He modeled a lifestyle that was totally committed to God. and by following His example, His disciples would be transformed from the inside out. In time, they would model total commitment to God and transform their followers.

5. Jesus Modeled What He Taught

The things that thou hast heard of me among many witnesses, the same commit thou to faithful men, who shall be able to teach others also (2 Timothy 2:2).

Jesus prepared His followers by example to be fishers of men. He taught them faith by walking on water and love by dying on the cross. He showed how to be forgiving through His treatment of the woman caught in adultery and how to be tolerant through His interaction with the Samaritan woman. He demonstrated servanthood by washing His disciples' feet.

6. Jesus Focused on Potentials, Not Problems

He said, " I will make you fishers of men." He did not say to James and John, "You have bad tempers. I don't want you." He did not say to Peter, "You are so brash and always talking out of turn, I can't use you." Or to Thomas, "I can't use you because you won't believe Me anyway." Or to Judas, "You are going to betray Me, so I won't count you in." Jesus looked beyond the frailties and the weaknesses of His disciples.

It is easy to think, "I am just a Sunday School teacher," but don't take this role lightly. You may never see the fruits of your ministry; one plants, another waters, and God gives the increase (see 1 Corinthians 3:9). So set your focus on the potential of your students. Know that as you build quality in your students by pouring your life into them, by looking at their potential, and by giving quality time, you will change their lives.

The Teaching-Learning Process

Good teachers focus their teaching methods on the goal of awakening the spirit of each learner so they can be responsive to God (1 Corinthians 2:14). This involves knowing something about the teaching and learning process. Teaching is more than presenting information. I firmly believe that if the student hasn't learned, the teacher hasn't taught! To empower, teachers reach through the natural process of learning and the various methods of teaching in order to foster spiritual growth.

1. The Holy Spirit as Helper

Jesus told His disciples,

> "He will guide you into truth; for He will not speak on His own authority, but whatever He hears He will speak: and He will tell you things to come. He will glorify Me, for He will take of what is Mine and declare it to you." (John 16:13–14 NKJV)

Therefore Christian teachers understand that the Spirit empowers them to teach for changed lives. This is crucial, because for students to be empowered, teachers must first be empowered by the Holy Spirit. For teaching to result in genuine life changes, both teachers and learners must give the Holy Spirit His rightful place in the learning process. While I was at Evangel Temple, the goal was to teach and learn spiritual truths, not just intellectual facts. We tried to strengthen the pupils' inner motivation and change their attitudes and behaviors. We did this with the help of the Holy Spirit, who is the only one who can motivate genuine and permanent life changes.

The Holy Spirit uses God's Word in a powerful way to change lives. The more we bring students into direct contact with God's Word and help them wrestle with its meaning, the more exciting, life-changing learning will occur. Real spiritual growth takes place when the teacher relies on the Holy Spirit for teaching power and when learners rely on the Holy Spirit for learning power. Allow the Holy Spirit to be an active, powerful part of your teaching. Include Him in your planning. Talk to Him about specific learner needs. Encourage the students to talk with God about their responses to His Word and about their personal needs.

2. The Teaching Cycle

What, specifically, is the teaching process? What elements are involved? The teaching process is composed of the following cyclical steps:

a. Approach. The approach is the teacher's introduction to the lesson. During the approach the teacher focuses on the students' interests in the topic or theme for the Bible study. The approach should arouse interest, involve the students, and lead naturally into the lesson study. The students should be made "ready" to discover biblical answers to personal needs. Some methods for the approach are life-situation stories, open-ended stories, current events, brainstorming, agree-disagree questions, skits, role playing, or interviews.

b. Bible Explorations. In this step the teacher guides the students to explore God's point of view in the Scriptures. Students must know what the Bible teaches before they can apply scriptural truths to their own lives. Methods used in Bible exploration may include group Bible studies, team Bible panels, lectures, dramas, or skits.

c. Life Application. In application, the teacher provides opportunities for learners to discuss, demonstrate, and practice God's principles for their life situations. It is essential that the students have a chance to apply kingdom principles to contemporary situations. Learners should be guided to focus on specific areas of personal need. Methods to achieve life application are buzz groups, circle response, thought-provoking questions, case studies, self-evaluations, writing projects, and personal questionnaires.

d. Assuming Responsibility. It is not enough to know kingdom truth or even see its implications for life. The teacher's goal is to lead learners to an understanding that they are responsible for the truth revealed. The teacher must help students to see that unless the Word of God is applied in their lives, the seed is lost in the infertile ground of the heart. Methods for encouraging responsibility are written reminders, individual and group projects, prayer-and-share groups, or keeping diaries.

e. Decision. Students must be led to their own "decision" concerning the application of the lesson truth in their lives. That is, guided by their teacher, the students should decide on specific ways to respond to a lesson. Most importantly, the teacher should pray that students make the decision to obey the Word that will change their lifestyles. The teacher should also plan to follow up on students during the week with phone calls and on the following Sunday with group reports or personal conversation.

3. How Learning Becomes Effective

Learning is an active process in which the pupils are participating, interacting, and discovering God's truth for themselves. Learning is continuous because it is a steady, on-going process proceeding from the known to the unknown. It is also a disciplined process in which there is guidance, control, and authority. Christian learning is not simply obtaining Bible knowledge, but being empowered to express and live out kingdom teachings. Sometimes a teacher might assume that a student has learned because the lesson material has been covered. This is not always true. There must be a change in the student's attitude or behavior. Such a change must be evident before one can say with assurance that the pupil has "learned."

At the same time, we must recognize that there are different levels of learning.

a. The first level of learning is **cognitive.** This is the level of knowledge or information. On the cognitive level we come to know, understand, or recognize factual information. After students have participated in a series of stimulating learning activities, they will be able to know or to understand certain biblical truths. By the end of each session, they should know some new facts and truths.

Many Sunday school teachers typically focus on the cognitive level because the results are measurable. It is easy to determine whether students understand the truths presented or have learned facts they did not know before.

b. The second level is **affective.** The aim of affective learning is to feel. It encompasses our emotions or attitudes toward the information given to us. After students have participated in the planned learning activities of a session, they will be able to feel a certain response to a given truth. Students' attitudes about subjects influence their learning ability. Sometimes a teacher must help students change their feelings or attitudes about a subject before they can respond to a truth in a way that makes a difference in their lives. For example, middle or high school youth may have an open discussion about their bodies as the temples of the Holy Spirit and then evaluate their attitudes toward sexual abuse or promiscuity.

Success at the affective level of learning is harder to measure than success at the cognitive (knowledge) level. The best test of success of affective learning is a teacher's personal observations of attitude changes in the lives of the learners. To accomplish this, teachers needs more than in-class contact with their students.

c. The third level of learning is **behavioral.** The goal of the behavioral level is response. After working through the learning activities in one session, the students will be able to do something in a practical way to respond to a new truth. The best way for teachers to verify real change in learners' actions or responses is to observe them at church or in social situations. It takes time to assess these, but this practice is effective for teachers who are willing to give the time.

The greatest reason for failure to produce dramatic life changes through Sunday school is teaching stopping short of the behavioral level. Some students know and understand Scripture, and they even feel good about it, but they never do anything about it! As a result, their lives are not changed by the truths they learn, and Christians whose lives look just like those of unbelievers influence the world very little.

4. The Learning Process

Effective teachers understand how people learn. These are teachers who recognize that the more deeply students are motivated to think and feel, the more actively they will learn. The more actively they respond, the more they will learn. Teachers do not need to be discouraged if they see little outer change in the students, because external change may lag behind inner learning. Plateaus may come, and growth may seem at a standstill. Or there may be sudden spurts when decisive growth is apparent. Teachers can know that if they prayerfully do their best in presenting God's truth, God's Spirit will continue to work in the hearts of the students.

Students learn to apply truths to their lives through this step-by-step learning process:

    a. Students are introduced to facts or ideas that are new to them.

    b. Students relate these facts or ideas to something they already know, as they interact with their teacher and the divine Teacher (the Holy Spirit).

   c. As students relate new encounters and interactions to their previous experiences, their experiences widen and their understanding increases.

   d. Students' broadened experiences and increased understanding enable them to use the new learning to help meet their needs and solve problems in their lives.

5. The Learning Cycle

Learning is a cyclical process that takes place in five orderly steps.

a. Approach. In the first phase the students receive instruction concerning the learning activity. During the approach, the teachers set the tone for the entire teaching session. Thus, the approach phase of the learning cycle is essentially one in which the learners receive new information and instructions.

b. Explore. In the second phase the students need an opportunity to do some of their own investigation on the subject the class is studying. The students may examine the Scripture passage, use research materials to study the meanings of words or the historical background of the passage, or answer questions related to the Scripture. It is important that the learners, under the guidance of the teacher, think and explore the Word of God for themselves. In this way they learn the lesson firsthand and learn that they have personal access to the empowerment of the Holy Spirit.

c. Discover. In the third phase the teachers guide the students until they discover the meaning of the passage or the answer to the problem. The important part is that the students be allowed to participate directly in discovering a new idea or truth themselves. A truth becomes personal when the students have discovered it by exploring on their own. Through these learning experiences, the students recognize that the Scriptures can be understood through the enabling power of the Holy Spirit. To discover the Bible is to find out what the Bible means.

d. Appropriate (Apply). In the fourth phase the teachers guide the students to make the truth part of their daily lives. Students may get so caught up in the learning activities and their personal exploration that they may not even consider how the new truth will affect their daily living. To produce changed lives, the teacher must help pupils see how discovered truth applies in practical, concrete ways.

e. Assume Responsibilities. In this phase the learners assume the responsibility for the truth they have discovered by beginning to act on it and make specific life changes as a result of their discovery. Changing habits is difficult and sometimes painful, and we often resist even when we know our old way is wrong. When students reject change, good teachers start the learning process again and pray for guidance. The teachers may help the students take those steps, but it is up to the students to take the action and assume the final responsibility for learning. Through these life changes the students begin to conform to the image of Christ. There are no short-cuts to genuine learning. The teachers must guide, motivate, and care. The students must receive information, explore, discover, appropriate, and assume the responsibility.

Standards for Bible Study

Finally, consider the important subject of Bible study. The Bible is your teaching ministry's textbook. It should be studied according to a systematic plan, and portions of it memorized. Here are three reasons to study the Bible:

1. Jesus commanded His followers to teach the Bible. He told them to go and "make disciples . . . , teaching them to observe all things that I have commanded you" (Matthew 28:20 NKJV).
2. Jesus said, "If you love Me, keep My commandments" (John 14:15 NKJV).
3. The early church robustly taught the Scriptures.

Jesus and the Learning Cycle

The learning cycle can be illustrated through Jesus' teachings. The story of the rich young ruler (Matthew 19:16–22) reveals the techniques of the Master Teacher.

Phase 1: Approach. The young man was in the approach phase of learning when he was curious about how to obtain eternal life (v. 16). Jesus encouraged his interest by responding to a question the man asked (v. 17). Jesus focused his attention on the matter of the Ten Commandments as important for obtaining eternal life (v. 17). The ruler had not yet learned anything new, but he was ready to move to the next phase of learning, in which he could receive new information.

Phase 2: Explore. The young man was exploring when, in response to Jesus' statement about keeping the commandments, he replied, "Which ones?" (v. 18 NKJV). The exploring process continues through verses 19 and 20, where the ruler is still asking questions.

Phase 3: Discover. To discover the Bible is to find out what the Bible means. Jesus led the young man to the point of discovery with the words, "If you wish to be complete, go and sell your possessions . . . and come, follow Me" (v. 21).

Phase 4: Assume Responsibility. There is no record that the rich young ruler sold all he had or gave it to the poor or followed Christ. Thus it appears that he refused to assume responsibility for what he now knew to be true (v. 22). He refused to let the truth be a guide for his behavior. This action illustrates that a person may step out of the learning cycle at any point, for any reason.

Keep in mind that one may move through all five phases in one session or in a series of sessions. This story is but one example of how Jesus taught. Search the Scriptures for other examples of the Master Teacher and His methods. In the meantime, consider Jesus' teaching style in the following Scriptures: John 8:1–11, Luke 5:1–11; Luke 24:13–35; Matthew 14:22–23.

Again, the Bible is your textbook. A hit-or-miss, unorganized approach can cheat students out of the truths God wants to share and build into their lives. I believe that when the following five standards of Bible study are applied, the result is a truly Bible-centered teaching ministry.

Standard 1: A Solid Bible Curriculum. "Your Word I have hidden in my heart, that I might not sin against You" (Psalm 119:11 NKJV).

A curriculum must be developed so that the students are given a systematic study of the entire Bible over a period of three years. Students must commit to memory specifically assigned Scriptures to "treasure the Word" in their "heart." Several outstanding curriculum programs exist that reflect the realities of the urban setting. I recommend the program from Urban Ministries Incorporated in Chicago and the Echo curriculum from David C. Cook Publishing Co. of Colorado Springs particularly useful.

Standard 2: An Emphasis on Biblical Evangelism: "You shall receive power when the Holy Spirit has come upon you; and you shall be witnesses to Me" (Acts 1:8).

All teachers should be trained and actively involved in seeking to lead students to Christ, using an approach appropriate to the age level. Biblical evangelism is an essential part of an effective Bible teaching ministry.

Standard 3: A Student-Concerned Focus. Urban educators must be interested in making disciples out of students. A disciple will go beyond just acquiring information and make an earnest attempt to take responsibility for what is learned.

Too often teachers become so concerned with meeting students' spiritual needs that they forget the students are whole people with a multitude of needs. The Gospels reveal Jesus ministering not only to people's spiritual needs but also to their other needs, using a holistic approach. It can be hard for people to respond to a spiritual truth when they are consumed by other, seemingly more pressing, needs. Therefore teachers must have in view ways for physical needs such as food, clothing, shelter, and health to be met.

Wise Bible teachers learn to recognize and use the needs of the students to help them learn the truths of God's Word. If a student has the need to achieve, help him or her to do something successful during the session.

Some general needs relate to all age levels, but each level also has specific needs that must be understood and planned for in a Bible-teaching ministry. Teachers should study the characteristics of their students' age range and learn responses to these specific needs.

Furthermore, students have individual needs based on their personalities and lifestyles. Teachers will learn these needs as they become friends with each student in the class.

How does all this relate to a student-concerned focus? Evaluate your classroom on this standard. Are your team members aware of the basic needs of their students? Is your Bible study designed to help your students meet their needs? Here are a few items to consider in ensuring that your Sunday school ministry is learner focused:

a. Discuss this standard. See if you can identify any ways in which not meeting your students' needs have decreased effectiveness of your Bible study ministry. Some examples are hot and stuffy classrooms, decreased concentration, no learner involvement, lack of attention, boredom, and disruption.

b. Brainstorm during the teaching time some ideas for helping to meet your students' basic needs.

c. Write down three or four of the ideas. Start the next week implementing at least two of these ideas. Then evaluate the impact of these changes on the quality of your Bible teaching.

Standard 4: An Emphasis on Learner Involvement: "And let our people also learn to maintain good works, to meet urgent needs, that they may not be unfruitful"(Titus 3:14 NKJV).

Involve the students in the Bible study. Assist them in making positive life changes based on God's Word. It is a common error to focus teaching on what the teacher does rather than on observing what the student does. Teachers can study, prepare, and receive a great blessing from Bible teaching, but the students can sit passively and listen and be robbed of the joy of discovering Bible truths for themselves. Therefore, there are two essential points to bear in mind regarding student involvement:

a. The importance of changed lives. An important goal of the teaching/learning cycle is grasping the importance of teaching the Bible in order to change lives. But this alone is not enough to change lives in the classroom. The teacher must determine the most effective teaching method that will take the students' needs and characteristics into consideration to produce positive, measurable change in their lives.

b. Involve the learner. People learn best when they are involved in the teaching/learning process. Involvement means to draw learners in as participants. It means that learners will be active during the Bible teaching experience. I believe that the more involved the student is in the teaching/learning process, the more they'll comprehend. The following figures demonstrate the importance of involvement in the classroom:

- We retain 10% of what we *read.*
- We retain 20% of what we *hear.*
- We retain 30% of what we *see and hear.*
- We retain 70% of what we *say.*
- We retain 90% of what we *say and do.*

The figures clearly show that involving the students' senses leads to greater learning experiences. For the adult Bible student, such involvement may be activities that include group discussions (e.g., buzz groups), where they examine a verse or chapter to discover biblical principles and relate them to a Christian lifestyle. Teenagers need to be involved in finding, reading, and answering questions from Scripture and then responding to what God's Word says to them. Children can be directly involved through reading, memorizing, and singing God's Word and through expressing their response with art, drama, and other creative activities. Moreover, children may be introduced to firsthand experiences with the Bible. Even if they cannot read for themselves, they need to see the Bible in the classroom, listen to the teacher reading it, and memorize appropriate sections. All students should have a firsthand experience with the Bible every Sunday.

As we have already seen, preparing a lesson and involving the student are tasks that should not be taken lightly. They require time, creativity, and resourcefulness. Involvement curriculum for young children needs to include activity centers where they can experience God's wonders. Bible-learning activities can help them explore and do something about a Bible passage or concept. Involving adults means having something for them to see during a lecture block, something for them to write during discussions circles, and some creative way for them to explore Bible passages.

Standard 5: Familiarity with the Learning Process: "But be doers of the word, and not hearers only, deceiving yourselves" (James 1:22 NKJV).

All teachers and leaders should receive training in the steps of the learning process. This process helps the teacher to see how to move a learner from just knowing the Bible to acting upon its teachings.

Standard 6: The Teacher's Role. "Pay close attention to yourself and to your teaching; persevere in these things; for as you do this you will insure salvation both for yourself and for those who hear you"(1 Timothy 4:16 NASB).

As a guide, the teacher encourages the student. As a model, the teacher's life exemplifies scriptural principles. As a friend, the teacher find outs what the needs of the students are and is sensitive to them.

Summary

The purpose of this chapter has been to provide urban church educators with a basic introduction to educational methods. We have examined the methods used by Jesus Christ, the Master Teacher. We also explored the practical steps involved in the teaching-learning process. Finally, we have considered criteria for establishing effective Bible study.

Questions for Discussion

1. Describe the various methods Jesus used in his teaching ministry. How would you compare your own method with them?
2. Discuss the learning cycle. How important is it to the teaching ministry of your church?
3. Describe the five standards the author presents for effective Bible study.
4. How important is Bible study in the process of empowering people to be achievers? Explain.
5. Describe what you believe are the strengths and the weaknesses of the Bible study program at your church.

The African-American Male Mentoring Program

The Reverend Carl Manuel Jr. is the part-time director of the African-American Mentoring Program for Guilford Technical Community College (GTCC) in Greensboro, North Carolina. He is also the senior pastor of St. Paul's AME Church in Mount Airy, North Carolina, a city recognized as the setting of the 1960s television sitcom *The Andy Griffith Show.*

Today Pastor Manuel is concerned for Mount Airy's increasingly negative perception of young African-American males as street loiterers. The situation caused Pastor Manuel to ask himself whether there was anything his congregation could do. "The Lord impressed upon me," he said, "to do something to prevent young males from just hanging around and getting into trouble." He is quick to point out that "in the major urban centers in the United States, African-American males are an endangered species."[1] His vision is to get young men into a program that stimulates them positively before they are lured into a negative, or what he calls self-destructive, pattern of behavior.

Pastor Manuel turned his attention to middle school (ages eleven to thirteen), and he made a conscious decision to develop a mentoring program for boys who are motivated to succeed and were not having behavior problems at school or at home.

"I believe there are a number of programs that respond to the needs of at-risk boys, but few that address boys who are self-motivated," Manuel says. "By self-motivated, I mean specifically boys who in general exercise good behavior, are not involved in drugs, have a solid academic performance at school, and are inclined to attend church regularly. You see, I believe the self-motivated lad is neglected in the current dialogue about African-American boys. My program will provide positive male role models so that these boys are kept on the straight and narrow."

He is concerned that in the absence of positive role models and constructive things to do, there is a higher chance for these boys to get into trouble.

Pastor Manuel started the program in his church about three years ago. Twenty-five boys expressed interest and had to go through a screening or qualifying process before they were accepted. The boys who qualified were presented with the purpose of the program and the following list of activities:

1. Lessons in Christian living involving real life situations
2. Goal-setting activities and career options
3. Recreation and cultural activities such as sports, museums, and movies
4. Service projects such as anti-drug campaigns, tutoring programs for peers who need help, or any other service project they are interested in
5. Motivational activities for spiritual enrichment such as High IQ Bowl games that enhance biblical knowledge
6. Assisting in developing a set of recommendations for the local church on how they, as African-American males, perceive the role of the church in improving their situation

Four male mentors were screened by Pastor Manuel and joined the program. The program met on Wednesday nights from six to nine o'clock. Each mentor had six to eight boys in his group. While parents have no official role in the program, they are supportive. Some parents cannot get directly involved because of work schedules, but others are able to help in various ways, such as providing transportation to activities and events. As the program grew, an annual banquet was added—held at the church, with a leading African-American figure in the community as the speaker. This event also serves to promote the program to the broader community.

Pastor Manuel believes he has seen results from his mentoring program. He observes that in general the participants have improved academically. Many parents report that the boys are conscientious and are doing well in school. There are evaluation forms for both the parents and the boys.

He also observes that as the boys interact with positive male role models, their self-esteem improves. "A major problem with our boys is that they have low expectations and poor self-esteem," says Pastor Manuel. He believes that one of the program's strengths is that the boys build confidence. Another strength is the exposure the boys receive to a variety of career options, including politics, business, and law. "I believe the exposure to the almost infinite variety of jobs and opportunities expands the boys' level of awareness and this raises the level of expectation," Manuel says. He believes it will succeed if the boys can be identified early and given direction from a positive male role model.

Yet Manuel also sees weaknesses in the program. He says, "There really is not enough time to give the boys the individual attention I think they need." He believes one-on-one attention gets neglected because the program meets just one night a week, and these meetings usually have a planned agenda. He also feels that the goals should be reassessed and that the evaluation process can be improved. On that score, I would like to see the program expand its evaluation to include people in the larger community and expand the organization to include other church leaders.

Despite its weaknesses, I believe the program is important because it focuses on boys who are well motivated and not at risk. In that regard, it is a solid program that can meet a neglected need in the African-American community.

Pastor Manuel offers ten core mentoring principles he has learned through his work in the program:

1. Set standards for achievement, allow for mistakes.
2. Encourage goal setting, short-term and long-term.
3. Emphasize strengths.
4. Notice and affirm special characteristics.
5. Encourage the expression of ideas, even if they are different from your own.
6. Encourage and help the boys to become aware of their own decision-making process.
7. Help the boys to face the consequence of their behavior.
8. Encourage discussions around beliefs and interests.
9. Encourage personal responsibility.
10. Encourage and ask the boys to use their special talents or interests to encourage others.

Reverend Carl Manuel Jr. may be contacted at St. Paul's AME Church, 321 North, South Street, Mount Airy, North Carolina, at 336-789-5853.

CHAPTER 7

Struggling for Knowledge

The Legacy of African-American Education

In 1933, the noted African-American historian and educator Carter G. Woodson commented on the deplorable state of education for "the negro race" in America, saying that it promoted the myth of "negro" inferiority and white superiority. He went on to say,

> When you control a man's thinking, you do not have to worry about his actions. You do not have to tell him not to stand here or go yonder. He will find his "proper place" and will stay in it. You do not need to send him to the back door. He will go without being told. In fact, if there is no back door, he will cut one for his special benefit. His education makes it necessary.[1]

Dr. Woodson's point is convincingly argued in his book *The Mis-Education of the Negro*, in which he provides a scathing critique of the fundamental principles of education for "negroes" in the 1930s and 1940s. He argues that the whites' control of the content of education for the "negro" reinforced self-hate and promotes inferiority. Such a system of education cannot continue to exist because it would not facilitate progress for the "negro race."

Education for African-Americans is a crucial factor in their struggle for empowerment, liberation, and justice. Today this

issue is as important as it was in Woodson's day. In urban centers, public education is a major concern. Poor test scores, violence, gangs, and drugs have turned too many public schools
into war zones where metal detectors and police searches keep
the peace. The high dropout rate and the inferior education
urban children typically receive are all well documented.[2]

To understand the importance of urban church education
and the need for an empowerment approach, we must look at
the history of the African-American quest for religious instruction. I say "religious instruction" simply because it was the primary type of learning slaves received from colonial times until
well after the Civil War and Reconstruction. This chapter looks
briefly at three crucial periods in the history of African-Americans: slavery (1619–1865), Reconstruction (1866–1877), and
twentieth-century developments. We will review the efforts of
white denominations to provide religious instruction to slaves,
the barriers to that instruction, the efforts by the black independent church, and the changes that occurred with the breakdown
of legal segregation. The focus will be particularly on the efforts
of the African-American independent church.

Slavery Era, 1619–1865

There is no way to describe the horror of the American system of chattel slavery. Until the Fourteenth Amendment was rat-
ified after the Civil War, the United States Constitution provided
that African-Americans be counted as only three-fifths of a person in the censuses that determined the number of representatives to Congress. The idea that one human being could consider
another human being less human—as property or as having
three-fifths of a soul—is atrocious and incomprehensible.

Still, slavery was not invented in the southern colonies. It
was common in the ancient world. But the type of slavery that
prevailed in North America was unique in its brutality. Societies
in antiquity regarded the slave as human. In many situations,
such as in the Greco-Roman world, slaves could work off their

debt and secure freedom within a specified period of time. By contrast, the chattel slavery in America regarded the slave as a non-being, as property like a horse or cow. The fact that it lasted from 1619 to 1865—nearly two and a half centuries—with the sanction of the church and as a normal and accepted part of society is simply mind-boggling!

The history of African-American education begins in this horrendous situation. The attention for a long while was focused only on religious instruction because the attitude was widespread that educating slaves in other ways was unacceptable. This attitude prevailed both during colonial times and after the nation was established. For example, in the southern states it was illegal to teach slaves to read. And, in their view, futile: John C. Calhoun, a slave owner who served as vice president of the United States and afterward became a U.S. senator, was typical as he passionately argued that slaves did not possess the intellectual capability to learn, so education was a waste of time.

One of the earliest efforts to educate slaves was sponsored by the Society for the Propagation of the Gospel, a London-based organization established in 1701. The purpose of the society was to bring religious instruction to "Indians" (Native Americans) and slaves. The society's effort among the Indians was only marginally successful, so the focus shifted to the slaves. Thomas E. Leland notes that "by 1731, Rev. E. Taylor of St. Andrew's Parish, near Charleston, South Carolina, was not only giving religious instruction to blacks, but also was teaching them elementary subjects of secular education."[3]

Because the society had strong ties to the Church of England, there was widespread hostility against it in America. Yet it persisted in its efforts. Colleen Birchett mentions that the society "became the single most significant agency for the religious activity of negroes in the south."[4] But given the strong opposition, it is not surprising that, as Leland explains, "with the onset of the Revolutionary War, the Society's connection with the American colonies was severed."[5] With the vacancy left by the society, the burden shifted to denominations to fill the void.

The Presbyterian effort, led by the Reverend Charles C. Jones, established "plantation missions" to provide religious instructions for slaves. Albert J. Raboteau states,

> Ideally, the aim of the plantation mission was to create a "bi-racial community" of Christian masters and slaves.... The missionary's ideal picture of a Christianized master-slave relationship contributed to the southern myth of the benevolent planter-patriarch presiding benignly over his happy black folk.[6]

In 1834 Jones wrote an instructional catechism called "A Catechism for Colored People," and then in 1842 he wrote a book called *The Religious Instruction of Negroes in the United States*. In both works Jones articulates the view that good Christian slaves ought to be obedient to their masters and should honor them according to the commands of the Holy Scriptures. Therefore, the basic instruction that slaves were receiving taught that God willed Negroes to be slaves and disobedient slaves were out of God's will. William B. Seabrook, a prominent slave owner in South Carolina, saw the benefits of religious instruction that taught the "duties of slaves and rights of masters."[7] Seabrook rejected the idealism of Jones's Christian master-slave relationship.

The Methodists' and the Baptists' efforts for religious instruction for the slaves looked similar to the work of the Presbyterians. For example, in 1833 a Methodist minister named William Capers developed a catechism for the slaves that dealt with the basic tenets of the Christian faith.

However, these denominations were divided over this issue. By the mid-1840s, the division within the churches over the issue of religious instruction for slaves was growing deeper and deeper. The rebellion led by Nat Turner in 1831 in South Hampton, Virginia, was cited as proof that the religious instruction of the slaves would lead to rebellion and a disruption of the southern way of life. This division led to open schism. The Methodist Church split in 1844 and the Baptists in 1845. In summary, Leland states,

As the Abolitionist movement organized and later gained momentum in the 1830's and 1840's, Baptist and Methodist, as well as the Presbyterian Church, found themselves in an uncomfortable position. Because the abolitionists accused southern churches of neglecting slaves, the Presbyterian Church, along with others, felt the need to refute this charge. On the other hand, southern planters were not prepared to tolerate much attention being given to the instruction of slaves. In the end, planters won the day and the religious instruction of slaves lost much of its integrity.[8]

During the era of slavery, the obvious hindrance to providing religious instruction was that, as Leland says,

because slaves were considered property like horses, cows, and other possessions, there was little sustained motivation for slave owners to take the time to improve [provide religious instruction] this property unless a guaranteed return on the investment could be seen.[9]

And within the antebellum South, where slavery was an essential part of the economic and social structure, no such return was feasible.

Another hindrance was a moral question: Did slaves have a soul? Anthropologist-theologian James O. Buswell III offered this explanation:

The great dilemma which existed from the beginning of slavery in the New World until the Civil War was the fundamental opposition of the principles of Christianity to the institution of slavery itself. For the slave holder it took form initially in the stark question as to whether or not the conversion or baptism of his slave (which many had considered soulless) necessitated any change in his status as a slave.[10]

The response of the slave owners was a resounding no! The baptism or conversion of slaves did not change their legal status as property.

To ease their consciences, the slaveholders, in collaboration with lawmakers, passed slave codes[11] legally stipulating that

Christian conversion or baptism did not change the legal status of slaves as property. Also, the slave owners collaborated with the church denominations to teach that slaves really did not have souls, that essentially slavery as an institution was humane and, in fact, the will of a sovereign God.[12]

In the end, religious instruction left little or no major impression upon the majority of slaves. Ironically, the Bible, which is fundamentally a book about God's liberating and empowering activities in human affairs, was used by the church as an instrument to perpetuate bondage.

Reconstruction, 1866–1877

During the period after the Civil War there was significant progress toward religious instruction for the former slaves. That was in large part because the independent church became the center of identity and community for former slaves during Reconstruction. The church was the only institution over which the ex-slaves had any control or ownership. Moreover, because of white oppression, injustice, and racism, African-Americans were psychologically despondent. Although they were affected by the heat of white oppression and injustice, Franklin Frazier says, "Nevertheless, he [the African-American] could always find an escape from such, often painful, experiences within the shelter of his church."[13] C. Eric Lincoln said unequivocally, "The black church has no challenger as the cultural womb of the black community."[14] And Joseph Durham insightfully says, "The black church serves a number of purposes. Historically, it served as our school, our concert hall, our lecture platform, and a forum of community issues."[15] My vision is to see the African-American urban church, in this same spirit, rise to reassert itself as the educational citadel of the community, to respond to the problems in the community with empowering programs.

With the occupation of the South by the northern troops, northern free blacks and white philanthropic groups began to establish schools. The ex-slaves had been legally freed by the Emancipation

Proclamation, but they were economically destitute and, generally speaking, uneducated. To fill this void, chaplains from the northern armies established classes. The American Missionary Society, established in the North, also set up schools. Carter G. Woodson wrote that "by 1868, the Society had as many as 632 missionaries and teachers working among the blacks."[16] In fact, the society had helped establish a day school for the ex-slaves in Hampton, Virginia, as far back as 1861, when the war was just beginning.

One of the major contributors to the general progress of the former slaves was the Freedman's Bureau, established in 1865. This agency was responsible for providing assistance in the form of providing food, clothing, and employment and establishing schools.[17] In fact, regarding the Freedman's Bureau, Leland comments, "during five years of its existence, this bureau established 4,279 schools in the South with a total number of 9,307 teachers and 247,333 students."[18]

It should be noted that because of federal funding, the Freedman's Bureau did not establish religious schools. However, there occurred a unique integration between religious instruction done in a Sunday school format and secular instruction done in a church-school setting. Soon a very practical issue arose: The former slaves did not possess the skills of reading and writing and, therefore, neither Bible study nor any other kind of religious instruction was possible. The church proved to be an invaluable contributor to the religious instruction of the ex-slaves. Leland points out, "It was in these church/school houses that many negroes received their first training in books."[19]

The church provided social cohesion and identity for the former slaves, without which they would have undoubtedly been overcome by the brutal realities of prejudice and discrimination. In this setting, the African Methodist Episcopal Church greatly contributed to the advancement of education and religious instruction. It established Sunday school classes, day schools, and even four colleges. The Baptists also established Shaw University in Raleigh, North Carolina, in 1865 and Morehouse College in Atlanta in 1867.

Another important hindrance during the era of Reconstruction was the lack of resources to meet the massive demand for religious instruction of the former slaves. Facilities were inadequate; church-schools were little more than shacks or run-down barns. Untrained ministers and teachers as well as a lack of books and other educational resources set the stage for failure. Whatever progress was made had only a slight impact on the general situation of blacks. Near the end of Reconstruction, white reaction to the apparent gains of former slaves was hostile and often violent. The rise of white supremacy groups such as the Ku Klux Klan, coinciding with the withdrawal of northern troops, led to a regression for the ex-slave. There were many laws and codes like the so-called Black Codes and the famous Jim Crow laws that sought to enslave the minds as well as the bodies of black people.

Then, with the Supreme Court decision of *Plessy vs. Ferguson* in 1896, "separate but equal" became the law of the land. This established the philosophy of the inferiority of black people in terms of educational institutions that Carter G. Woodson lamented. It would not be until 1954, with the ruling in *Brown vs. Board of Education of Topeka*, that equal educational opportunity was offered to African-Americans.

Despite violent racism, inadequate facilities, and insufficient resources, the ex-slave continued to push toward education. James Anderson said that "former slaves were the first among native southerners to depart from the planters' ideology of education and society and to campaign for universal, state-supported education."[20] In addition to pushing for universal and public education, blacks established churches that offered Sunday school programs. For example, in the years that followed Reconstruction, the First African Baptist church in Richmond, Virginia—which was built by ex-slaves—established a school in the church basement. With great insight, Anderson says, "Blacks emerged from slavery with a strong belief in the desirability of learning to read and write.... It was a whole race trying to go to school. Few were too young and none too old to make the attempt to learn."[21]

It should also be noted that the Freedman's Bureau provided needed resources to build public schools for educating ex-slaves. The agency was also instrumental in establishing Howard University in Washington, D.C., in 1867. In 1870, another organization, the American Missionary Association, established 157 common schools throughout the South.

During the period from the 1870s through the 1890s, wealthy white individuals contributed money toward establishing common schools and colleges for blacks. In addition, white philanthropists such as Julius Rosenwald, Robert C. Ogden, and George Foster Peabody established foundations and endowments to support black colleges such as Tuskegee and Hampton institutes. Because of this philanthropy, colleges established earlier by white religious denominations grew stronger at this time, such as Cheyney State University (started in 1834 by the Quakers) and Lincoln University (started in 1854 by the Presbyterians), both in Pennsylvania.

Yet, in spite of the efforts of wealthy white individuals, philanthropic organizations, and white denominations, perhaps the most commendable action was the fact that blacks themselves were making tremendous sacrifices to financially support education. Blacks in the South were earning just enough wages to survive during this period. Anderson writes, "Various studies at the time revealed the extremely low incomes of those rural black families. Studies of black farm families who were chiefly tenants and sharecroppers showed that few were able to earn beyond what was required for bare subsistence."[22] Nevertheless, these sharecroppers collected pennies, nickels, and dimes to support and establish their own schools. A good example is Jones County, Texas, where, in 1917, blacks did not have a school and the county was slow to respond, so the blacks built their own school to meet their immediate educational needs. Anderson explains, "With minimal aid from the public school authorities, the black community of Jones County . . . succeeded in building a schoolhouse 'valued at ten thousand dollars.'"[23]

Shifts in the Twentieth Century

At the turn of the century, there was a passionate debate between the scholar W. E. B. DuBois and the educator Booker T. Washington. On the one hand, DuBois argued that a talented tenth must arise among blacks to engage in scholastic and intellectual efforts and to enter professions that were previously off limits to them. On the other hand, Washington argued that blacks needed jobs and vocational training; in a speech at the Atlanta Exposition of 1895, he eloquently said that blacks and whites can be as separate as the fingers are on a hand but in areas of mutual progress become one. This debate raged within the context of the general culture's move toward segregation.

It was also in this context that the Great Migration began. Thousands of blacks from the South traveled to northern cities during the 1920s and 1930s seeking jobs and educational opportunities. In the South, the *Plessy vs. Ferguson* decision, which had established "separate but equal," had deep effects on society. It damaged black strides for better education because, although separate, they certainly were not equal. Black public schools in the South were inadequate in terms of facilities, supplies, and basic resources. White legislators did not see the need to fund public schools in black communities even though white schools were funded. The equipment and textbooks used in black schools were old, worn-out, hand-me-downs previously used by whites.

The situation in the North into which the blacks were migrating was not much better. Black schools located in the cities typically were poorly funded. Yet, in spite of the deplorable conditions, there arose black leaders who went on to college and black athletes who excelled in sports. Some black schools made a name for themselves, such as Paul Laurence Dunbar High School in Little Rock, Arkansas, and Dunbar High School in Washington, D.C., and also in Baltimore, Maryland.

In 1954 the Supreme Court overturned the "separate but equal" doctrine in the landmark *Brown vs. Board of Education* decision. Thurgood Marshall, a graduate of Howard University Law

School, effectively argued that separate but equal was unconstitutional and morally reprehensible. The high court ruled that said the separate-but-equal doctrine adversely affected the minds and hearts of black children. With this decision, an era of desegregation busing began. There was tremendous social upheaval over the issue of busing white children to schools in black neighborhoods and black children to schools in white neighborhoods.

During the 1960s, as Dr. Martin Luther King Jr. was pressing for social changes and civil rights, the issue of education did not receive a lot of attention. The civil rights movement focused on voting, jobs, and accommodation issues more than educational issues. Then, in the 1970s and 1980s, the big question in education was affirmative action. Institutions of higher learning began to establish a quota for blacks in their schools of medicine, engineering, and law. The questions continue to this day as to whether race-based programs for scholarships and admittance are constitutional.

Finally, public education—ironically something that blacks struggled so hard to establish—has become disadvantageous, particularly for urban children. I believe that education can no longer be left in the hands of school administrators and bureaucrats, but must have the involvement of churches and businesses. The church must come alongside public schools and offer programs that booster achievement. There is a wonderful African proverb that says it takes a village to raise a child. Likewise, it takes an entire community to educate a child in urban America.

Summary

The process of educating African-Americans during the eras of slavery and Reconstruction was a tremendous struggle. To the white plantation owners who thought that slaves were inferior and incapable of learning, any education was regarded as a waste of time.

We have noted the efforts of various white organizations, individuals, and churches as well as the efforts of black independent churches toward education from the era of slavery to the present. This has obviously been only a brief sketch of the topic, yet it is a subject with which both blacks and non-blacks must be familiar.

Questions for Discussion

1. What do you think Carter G. Woodson meant when he said, "When you control a man's thinking, you do not have to worry about his actions"?
2. Describe the significant contribution of the black church in the education of black people during the period of Reconstruction.
3. John C. Calhoun argued that slaves did not possess the intellectual capability to learn, so education was a waste of time. Given the historical context, how would you counter Calhoun's argument?
4. Discuss the role of denominations such as the Methodists, Baptists, Presbyterians, and Quakers in the education of slaves. How would you evaluate their efforts?
5. Southern white slave owners permitted slaves to be taught the Bible in order to become more submissive and obedient. Do you think this introduction to the Bible was a factor in the Nat Turner rebellion of 1831 and the slave rebellions of the 1840s?
6. Discuss the impact of the Supreme Court decision in *Plessy vs. Ferguson* in 1896 on the education of black people in the United States during the next half-century.

A Congregational Response to Community Needs

Washington is sometimes called "the political capitol of the world." Political muscles are flexed in the halls of Congress and in offices all over the city. Very few of Washington's power elite would genuflect before the poor or the homeless. Yet, amid this political clout stands a church in the inner city that has decided to take up the towel of servanthood in order to reach its local community. This church is Greater Mount Calvary Holy Church.

As you travel along the 600 block of Rhode Island Avenue in northeast Washington, you soon become acutely aware of the impact of this church, which is led by co-pastors Bishop Alfred and Susie Owens. The church has been able to turn one city block that was depressed into a robust area that is now thriving. Greater Mount Calvary has taken seriously the words of Jesus in Matthew 5:13–14 that the believer is "the salt of the earth" and "the light of the world." With a plethora of relevant ministries to the poor, oppressed, and the homeless, and by purchasing numerous properties surrounding the church, Greater Mount Calvary is an oasis in a desert where despair, drugs, and crime too often prevail.

The church began as the Answer Chapel in May 1966 at 1430 Morse Street in northeast Washington, where it was founded by a nineteen-year-old evangelist named Alfred A. Owens Jr. The church had a modest beginning with membership ranging from nine to seventeen people. In 1971 this small congregation purchased a house and transformed the living room into a church sanctuary having a capacity of fifty. Later the church became a member of the Mount Calvary Holy Churches of America Inc. Then, in 1976 a merger with another church called Mount Calvary Holy Church raised the membership to about seventy. Gradually the congregation started to outgrow that location.

In 1983 the growing church made another move, this time purchasing a vacant church building on Park Road in northwest Washington.

There it added several ministries, including Calvary's Alternative to Alcohol and Drug Abuse (CATAADA).

Finally, the congregation in 1991 purchased the property formerly known as Evangel Temple at 610 Rhode Island Avenue in the Edgewood section of northeast Washington, which had a seating capacity of 2,000.

Greater Mount Calvary has striven to fulfill the Great Commission through reaching out to the surrounding community with the love of Jesus Christ and practical ministries that meet basic human needs with compassion. Its philosophy of ministry accepts the awesome responsibility of moving beyond the security of its sacred walls into the community of diverse needs and social ills.

The Edgewood community is experiencing the elements plaguing most inner-city urban areas: poverty, deficient education, and young people with low self-esteem. Edgewood also has a reputation for high drug traffic and high unemployment. Robbery and car thefts are common crimes; homicides result from drug deals gone bad, according to police.

The area is 90 percent African American and 8 percent Caucasian and has a growing Hispanic population. The last census data indicate there of the 858 households, only 272 were homeowners and 586 were renters. The city made an effort to improve the community in the early 1990s with the building of the Edgewood Shopping Center. Unfortunately, the presence of the shopping center has not resolved the unemployment problem that continues to plague Edgewood.

There are, however, signs of life in the community, not only in the many programs offered by Greater Mount Calvary Holy Church, but also in the Well Baby Clinic to assist unwed mothers and neighborhood watch programs.

The church has positioned itself as a resource center through such programs as a clothing and food bank, the drug and alcohol alternative, a ministry to the homeless, and an HIV/AIDS ministry. The church is teaching people how to improve their lives and to see a brighter vision of the future.

Bishop Owens is a warm and engaging person who has a passion for urban church ministry. He and his wife, Susie, have tackled the problems of the community head-on. He says that his view of urban ministry is "the church recognizing the needs of the surrounding community and responding to the need. In the Edgewood community the need is at times overwhelming."[24]

Bishop Owens believes that empowerment is a major motif for the urban church. "Empowerment is about equipping a person with the tools needed to succeed," he said. Therefore, he said, a church must endeavor to meet the needs of that community by proclaiming the gospel and by specific social ministry that empowers people. He urges churches that don't have a particular program in place, such as for AIDS/HIV, to support a church that does. He believes strongly in networking among churches because "there's no need to reinvent the wheel."

Among Mount Calvary's many ministries are the following:

1. CATAADA House. Started in 1983 and currently housed, like some of other programs, at the church's annex at 802 Rhode Island Avenue, this recovery program offers hope mixed with practical steps toward freedom from addictions. The format is modeled after Alcoholics Anonymous and Narcotics Anonymous, but CATAADA House adds an evangelistic aspect to the Twelve-Step Program. The program is staffed by people experienced in the field of addictive behavior.

2. HIV/AIDS Ministry. With compassion and truth, this fifteen-week peer counselor preparation training program focuses on prevention strategies with a comprehensive array of home care and other support services for those who are already infected. It also seeks to spread the message of risk reduction and prevention in the workplace, schools, youth groups, and homeless shelters. Participants undergo extensive training in AIDS/HIV awareness, substance abuse, and risk-reductive behavior.

3. Prison Ministry. Because the prison population has grown at such an alarming rate among young African American males, this ministry was established in 1987 with the vision of providing weekly visits to the local prison. Volunteers provide services such as family support, counseling, and Bible study. The ministry has been involved in the

Angel Tree Project, which provides food baskets, toys, and other gifts to the families of inmates.

4. Homeless Ministry. Homelessness is a major social problem in the District of Columbia, and shelters are often filled to capacity and understaffed. In 1989 the church began distributing food and blankets, but in 1992 began to assist people who did not have access to shelters. The program attempts to meet the whole person with spiritual guidance along with the physical goods. A unique feature, begun in 1995, is called the "Thanksgiving in July Celebration." This event brings homeless men, women, and children from off the streets to Calvary's complex, where they are provided a Thanksgiving-style meal and participate in a worship service.

5. The Food Bank. This ministry was established in 1991 and serves thousands of community residents each month, providing groceries without charge to senior citizens, unemployed people, low-income people, and the disabled. Using 1,550 square feet of operation and storage space, the five volunteer staff members serve an average of 500 people each week. Food distributions are made Monday through Wednesday and for four hours on Friday. The food bank obtains supplies from local and regional sources such as grocery stores and department stores.

6. The Clothing Boutique. The Calvary Clothing Boutique (CCB) was established in August 1995 with a vision to inspire and develop the spiritual and social growth of people in the community who needed decent clothing. The goal is to respond to immediate and urgent needs at no cost, yet clothing is not given out indiscriminately. People must come for a personal fitting. Departments that cater to women, men, and children, and alterations services are available.

7. Employment and Business Exchange. The primary mission of Calvary's Employment and Business Exchange (CEBE) is to help members obtain employment by providing information on available job vacancies, job counseling, coaching, and interview preparation. The program provides workshops to teach job seekers self-help skills and reliance on biblical principles about a solid work ethic. The vision is eventually to develop a full-time employment agency.

In summary, Greater Mount Calvary Holy Church is a unique church that has endeavored to empower the poor with a multitude of programs that provide people with "a hand up" approach to ministry instead of "a hand out."

For information about these programs and others, you may contact either Mr. Cedrick Brown or Bishop Alfred Owens Jr. at 202-529-4547.

CHAPTER 8

Reap What You Sow

Developing a Christian Philosophy of Education

While many urban educators do not have the time or inclination to study a Christian philosophy of education, it is important, particularly to churches that want to use education to empower. Modern culture is filled with a secular philosophy that denies eternal realities. Christians, however, embrace a biblical worldview. If urban church education is not grounded in a Christian worldview, it cannot achieve its goal. The Bible says that we reap what we sow. If we sow a philosophy that is secular, the harvest will be secularism. In the same way, if we sow a philosophy that is biblical, the harvest will be empowered spirituality.

While a Christian perspective seeks to empower humankind by dependence on a sovereign God, secularism seeks to do away with God and promote an individualistic society. Harry Blamires painted a grim picture of this cultural struggle when he wrote, a generation ago, "There is no longer a Christian mind. It is a commonplace that the mind of modern man has been secularized . . . but unfortunately the Christian mind has succumbed to the secular drift."[1]

The situation is even more complex today because secularism is by no means Christianity's only opposition. In modern society there are now multiple competing philosophies. Whether consciously or unconsciously, people tend to gravitate toward a particular philosophy that helps make sense of their existence. Fundamentally, everyone has a worldview or guiding set of assumptions about the world and life in general. No educational approach will be successful unless it first acknowledges that all students—children, teenagers, and adults—have their own views of their world, even if they don't articulate them.

The primary objective of empowering education is to develop within students a Christian worldview so that they can make critical assessments of the numerous unbiblical perspectives. In other words, empowering education develops a Christian mind. Its goal is the ability to think about life and the many issues that confront the individual from a Christian perspective.

Competing Worldviews

Several leading philosophies compete for the minds and attention of people who live in the city. These are not all the influences that affect them, but they are among the most prominent.

One philosophy that blocks the development of a Christian mind is *secular humanism*. Often this term is used, particularly by evangelicals, in a negative way. James D. Cunningham and Anthony C. Fortosis define secular humanism as "the condition or quality of being human . . . man as the focus of all values, beliefs and thinking, making man the measure of all things, thereby usurping God."[2]

James Hitchcock says that the person who adopts this view of the world is

> unable to see anything in the perspective of eternity, he cannot believe that God exists or acts in human affairs. Moral standards, for example, tend to be merely those commonly accepted by the society in which he lives, and he believes that everything changes, so that there are no enduring or permanent values.[3]

This view is perhaps the dominant worldview among people who live in the city, and its influence cannot be underestimated.

A second philosophy is *pragmatism*. Cunningham says pragmatism argues that "reality, value, truth and morality of ideas or events are determined in the light of their practical consequences ... a thing is true if it works."[4] In other words, pragmatism says, "If it works, use it!" The city can be a difficult place to live and work, so a view like pragmatism is particularly attractive. R. C. Sproul says, "In pragmatism truth is inevitably relativized.... if truth is determined by what works for the individual, then the test for truth ultimately becomes the individual himself."[5]

In the city, with its many different ethnic and cultural groups, conflict often occurs because individuals and groups determine what is "right for them," assuming that "right" is different for everyone. The problem with the pragmatic view of life is that this kind of relative truth cannot move beyond the subjective level of "what's right for you may not be what's right for me." Relativism and pragmatism have no room for any sense of ultimate or absolute.

A third competing philosophy is *existentialism*. The focus of existentialism is on feeling rather than rational thought. It focuses on humankind's feeling about their existence and the meaning of life. Because of this, Sproul calls existentialism "pessimistic."[6] The existentialist worldview is essentially negative and sees life itself as meaningless. In the city many have adopted this view of life because of the hard realities of poverty, crime, exploitation, and injustice. When city dwellers observe such harsh realities, they often ask, "What meaning is there to my existence?" This question is fundamental to all thinking people, yet it can become prominent in the harsh urban environment. When it leads to the frustrated conclusion, "What's the point anyway?" it becomes a dangerous and formidable view of life.

In addition to secular humanism, pragmatism, and existentialism, other competing philosophies get in the way of developing a Christian mind. *Agnosticism*, for example, is the view that one can neither affirm nor deny the existence of a personal God. In their attempt to be "objective," agnostics basically say that all the evidence presented for or against the existence of God is inconclusive. Another prevalent view is *atheism*. Atheists deny the existence of any deity. They believe that the universe came into existence by chance or has always existed and is sustained by resident, impersonal laws.

Marxism, which is not as widely understood by the general public, is another philosophy competing against a Christian worldview. Cunningham describes Marxism as "the political, economic, and religious theories of Karl Marx and Friedrich Engels, who interpreted history as a continuing economic class struggle. They believed ... the establishment of a classless society and communal ownership."[7] With its economic worldview and scathing critique of Western capitalism, Marxism has been particularly attractive to those who hold a liberation perspective. Liberation theology, particularly in Latin America, has used Marx's analysis of economic exploitation and class conflict to explain the miserable conditions of the poor and the oppressed. The typical urban dweller may not consciously use Marxist language but may recognize class distinctions and economic inequality.

My goal in outlining these philosophies is not to explain all conflicting worldviews but to point out the fact that the city dweller fights a battle. It is, as Dennis Peacocke says, "A battle to the death between ... competing world systems.... Although most ... are unaware of the immediacy of this battle, every single one of us is involved."[8] In other words, if empowering education principles are going to be effective in the urban situation, then educators must recognize that people who live in the city are confronted with very attractive views that are unchristian. It is important that empowering education not only be established on a Christian worldview but that it assist Christians in sorting out non-Christian worldviews.

Exploring a Christian Worldview

Empowering education seeks to develop a Christian mind in students. Robert Pazmiño describes the Christian mind when he defines a worldview as "a collection of underlying presuppositions from which one's thoughts and actions stem. A Christian world view is comprised of those fundamental Christian beliefs that most adequately describe the God-creation distinction and relationship. The challenge of this definition is integrating or relating Christian philosophy to everyday life. Often Christian education—whether formal or nonformal, Sunday school or day school—does not teach a Christian philosophy in a meaningful way that will influence the minds of adults and children. Pazmiño says, "The challenge for the Christian is to think 'Christianly' and rightly in all areas of human endeavor."[10]

Unfortunately, some so-called Christians have little or no regard for questions of ethics or integrity. What this means is that these Christians who do not integrate faith into action do not really have a Christian worldview. They continue to function with a secular worldview about the matters of life that really count.

For example, many Christians spend little time thinking about financial stewardship and are just as consumer oriented as non-Christians. They give little or no thought to discovering God's perspective on consumerism, as if God has nothing to say on this topic. Moreover, many Christians don't maintain a Christian worldview on such matters as shelter, food, family, and the basic necessities of life. They lack a biblical worldview that says God is aware of these areas of human concern and is taking care of them.[11] This does not mean that Christians should passively sit back and wait for God to organize their lives. Christians need to bring their concerns and cares to God, according to 1 Peter 5:7. My fear is that this important biblical truth is absent from the lives of some Christians. Living out the Christian faith involves more than just attending a church service on Sunday morning, for example. Thus, the real challenge of empowering education is the integration of a Christian worldview into everyday life.

Harry Blamires says a Christian mind is "a mind trained, informed, equipped to handle data . . . within a frame-work of reference which is constructed of Christian presuppositions. The Christian mind is the prerequisite of thinking."[12] The process of training the Christian mind involves prayer and instruction.

The biblical paradigm for this is found in two astounding statements of Paul. One is in 1 Corinthians 2:16: "But we have the mind of Christ." Paul meant by this the ability to think and to discern between things that are natural (things of this world) and things spiritual (things of the Spirit). The other key verse is Philippians 2:5: "Let this mind be in you, which was also in Christ Jesus." Here the apostle is talking about the mindset of servanthood and humility. Thus, the Christian mind is the ability to reflect on the things that are natural and those that are spiritual, and the willingness to assume the role of a servant, humbly submitting to God's commands.

Two examples of local churches that have attempted to empower with a Christian mind are Evangel Temple in Washington, DC, and Christ Covenant Church in Greensboro, North Carolina. As mentioned earlier, under the leadership of Bishop John L. Meares in the mid-1980s, Evangel Temple developed a lay Bible training school and a philosophy of education that emphasized the cultivation of a Christian mind. Evangel Temple School of the Bible was created to prepare students for lay ministry within a local church and to empower them to think Christianly about all aspects of their lives. The school was an evening program that offered affordable classes focusing on helping students to develop a Christian worldview.

Pastor David Longobardo of Christ Covenant Church wanted a new focus in the adult Sunday school program in 1994. The church had only incorporated adult Sunday school courses in its programs for short periods of time due to facility constraints. Moreover, those courses had focused on general themes and topics. In spring 1994 a new emphasis was implemented, focusing on instruction in books of the Bible and integrating biblical principles for practical Christian living. The goal of the program was to educate Christian minds that will encourage a Christian worldview. The result was that interest in adult Sunday school courses rose and the parishioners were challenged to think Christianly.

Many Christians have failed to develop a Christian mind or worldview because dualism has become a feature of our society. Dualism is the belief that there are two competing realities that are equally valid or true. Particularly in Western society, dualism has a tendency to compartmentalize things—secular versus the sacred, church versus state, religion versus politics, and so on. The roots of this dualism go back to the idealism of Plato in contrast to the realism of Aristotle. Plato argued that "truth and reality could be found only by turning from the material world to the world of the mind and ideas."[13] Thus, for Plato, the reality of the material world with its mountains, trees, and rivers are shadows cast by their ideal forms. In contrast to the ideal forms of reality by Plato, his most famous student, Aristotle, argued that reality is more than ideal forms; the "material world is reality."[14]

Some Christians side with Plato and affirm that it is the spirit world that is the true reality and not the tangible material world. Others say that reality is the tangible material world and so stand with Aristotle. Jack Layman says, "Idealism provides meaning without verification and realism provides verification without meaning."[15] However, the unifying element that brings together the dualism of idealism and realism is Jesus Christ. According to the apostle Paul, "in him all things consist" (Colossians 1:17). In Christ there is no longer any distinction between the sacred or the secular. For example, whatever we do—in work or play— matters to God and is to be done to His glory and is therefore sacred even if it does not appear to be overtly "religious."

A Christian Philosophy of Education

As demonstrated earlier, urban church educators must be aware of the influential philosophies that hinder developing a Christian worldview. Equally important, then, is the philosophy of the urban educators' ministry or school. A philosophy of Christian education is simply the set of guiding principles for an instructional program that is Christian based. Therefore our purpose here is to consider eleven points for constructing a philosophy of education that is Christ oriented.

1. A Christian philosophy of education is founded on the authority and reliability of the Bible as the only revelation of God concerning matters of faith, truth, and practice (2 Peter 2:19–21; John 17:17; 2 Timothy 3:16–17).

This means that the real authority in constructing a philosophy of education is the Bible. The Word of God is reliable concerning what is to be believed, what is to be regarded as truth, and what is to be practiced by believers. For example, the issue of curriculum material will lead the Christian educator to ask questions such as these: Does the material hold a high view of Scripture? Does it promote practices consistent with the historic Christian faith?

2. A Christian philosophy of education is founded on the trustworthiness of the teachings of Christ (Hebrews 1:1; John 14:6, 10–11).

What Jesus Christ taught about God, sin, and His sacrificial death are true. Jesus' words and His deeds are consistent and trustworthy. Believers can put the weight of their faith in Christ for salvation.

3. A Christian philosophy of education is founded on the recognition that the present-day ministry of Jesus Christ through the Holy Spirit empowers students to learn (John 14:16; 16:5–15; Acts 1:8; Hebrews 7:25).

This point acknowledges the reality of the Holy Spirit in the teaching process. It is the Holy Spirit who reveals the ministry of Jesus in the world today. The empowering presence of the Spirit illumines the mind of the student who is faithful and diligent to study.

4. A Christian philosophy of education is founded on clearly defined goals that are bibliocentric (John 5:39; Psalm 119:105; Proverbs 1:7; 16:3).

The Bible is the source on which objectives must be constructed. The urban church educator must keep in mind that goals for various programs must be in accordance with the Bible.

This point is important because there is a tendency to incorporate goals that are secular and to emphasize them to the exclusion of more biblical goals. For example, some circles emphasize quantitative goals such as attendance over more qualitative goals such as prayer.

5. A Christian philosophy of education is founded on the knowledge that all truth is the sole property of God. Therefore, any theory of knowledge that does not embrace the Bible and the trustworthiness of Christ is not true knowledge (Proverbs 8:22–31; Hebrews 11:3; Psalm 33:6; John 14:6).

Educators will encounter truth claims that come from sources outside the Scriptures. Yet Christian educators believe that the truthfulness of any source comes ultimately from God, who is truth. How do we recognize the truth? For Christians, the Bible is the source of truth.

6. A Christian philosophy of education is founded on the reality that truth is objective and transcendent as well as subjective and immanent. Christ stands as the center (Isaiah 55:8–9; John 1:1–4; Colossians 1:17).

Reality can be perceived objectively in the person of Jesus Christ. Urban church educators can rest in the assurance that they teach the truth so long as it is consistent with the Scriptures. Although God is outside of the reality of our world, in Christ He has entered our world, proclaiming liberation from it.

7. A Christian philosophy of education is founded on the moral imperative that a personal faith in and relationship with Christ are crucial to a fulfilled life (Acts 4:12; John 3:16; 10:10.)

Urban church educators must emphasize to their students that a satisfying and fulfilling life only comes by a personal relationship with Christ.

8. A Christian philosophy of education is founded on a proper relationship between the church, school, and family (Ecclesiastes 4:12; Isaiah 30:20–21; Psalm 78:1–8).

To educate students properly, their lives must have three crucial components: family, the school, and the church. All must work together. This is what lies behind the idea of a community raising a child. Each element—school, church, and family—has a specific God-given role.

9. A Christian philosophy of education is founded on the assumption that all students have the potential to learn and achieve (Matthew 10:24–25; Philippians 4:13; Proverbs 1:7; Joshua 1:8–9).

The urban church educator must develop a sense of confidence that all students have the potential to learn and to achieve. This assumption is crucial to empowering education.

10. A Christian philosophy of education is founded on the sovereignty of God (Isaiah 46:9–11; Philippians 2:13).

God is the ultimate sovereign of the universe. In other words, God has His own mind and is free to act in accordance to His will.

11. A Christian philosophy of education is founded on anthropology that understands that humankind is created in the image of God (Genesis 1:26–28; 2:7).

One problem that urban church educators confront is a lack of self-esteem in students. Thus, an emphasis on affirming the student's creaturehood in the image of God is important. Granted, the image of God is a theological concept that is hotly debated. However, the image is important for urban church educators because it incorporates humans' capacity to think, create, enjoy relationships, love, and transform their environment.

A Definition of Christian Education

Defining Christian education is a challenge because education can take on many forms. For example, imagine a continuum. On the one end there is formal learning in a school setting; on the other end, informal learning through life experience. Empowering education recognizes the value of both formal and informal education. In fact, empowering education understands that balance is important. A student can learn through life experience. Yet, as the proverb says, "Experience is the best teacher but the school of a fool." So formal schooling where students reflect and think about their life experiences is valuable. Considering the formal/informal continuum, Werner Graendorf offers a helpful definition of Christian education as

> a Bible-based, Holy Spirit-empowered (Christ-centered) teaching-learning process. It seeks to guide individuals at all levels of growth through contemporary teaching means toward knowing and experiencing God's purpose and plan through Christ in every aspect of living. It also equips people for effective ministry, with the overall focus on Christ the master educator's example and His command to make mature disciples.[16]

I am particularly attracted to this view of Christian education because it articulates six elements that are embraced by empowering educational principles:

- "Bible based" focuses on the content of education;
- "Holy Spirit empowered" focuses on the source of divine enabling for education;
- "Experiencing God's purpose and plan" focuses on the student's destiny and self-esteem;
- "In every aspect of life" focuses on biblical integration and application;
- "Equips people for effective ministry" focuses on training people for service; and
- "Make mature disciples" focuses on reproduction of Christlikeness in a disciple-making process.

We must point out that there are differences between methods of instructing children and adults. How we teach a child effectively will be different from the way we instruct an adult. On this matter, Patricia Cross says, "If adult education is a distinctive field of study at all, it is adult learners who make it so, and one of the best-known theories in adult education begins with the assumption that learning for adults is basically different from learning for children."[17]

This is important, because urban churches often approach instruction of adults and children the same way. Joseph Durham observes, "While it is true that most learn the same way, we cannot teach adults the same way we teach children. . . . All learners should be active, but for adults the action should be different."[18]

If similar methods are used, a common result is that adults become bored and uninterested in Sunday school classes. Urban church educators must remember that adults bring a wealth of prior experience and knowledge to the learning setting. It is always good to draw on that experience by asking questions and involving them in learning activities. Also, adult learners tend to be goal oriented. That is, they seek specific rewards and personal benefits from the learning setting. Finally, adults tend to want instruction that is practical and applicable to their lives.

Summary

The purpose of this chapter is not to provide an exhaustive discussion of the philosophy of education but rather to give educators a thumbnail sketch of the philosophical systems they are competing against. The fact is that many Christians are unaware of how much the contemporary culture has impacted their behavior. Unfortunately, for too long Christians have thought no differently from their unsaved counterparts. Harry Blamires refers to this as the lack of a "Christian mind." What he means is that far too many Christians have not cultivated a sound Christian worldview that informs their practice and beliefs. We have sought here to help the urban church educator better understand and prepare to confront city dwellers with programs that cultivate a Christian worldview. The chapter concludes with eleven points for constructing a philosophy of education.

Questions for Discussion

1. Do you agree or disagree with the author's statement that "for too long Christians have thought no differently from their unsaved counterparts"? Explain, giving specific examples.
2. Discuss the author's contention that secularism has a major influence on the lives of Christians and on non-Christians.
3. Do you agree with the author that the urban church educator needs to teach a Christian worldview to students? Explain your answer.
4. Explain the eleven points for a philosophy of Christian education. How would you instill these points into your ministry of Christian education?
5. Evaluate the author's definition of Christian education. What are its strengths and weaknesses?
6. Write your own definition of Christian education and contextualize it for your particular situation.

Conclusion

The motto of urban church education is "educational empowerment equals liberation." The city is a particularly difficult place for ministry because of the great diversity of social and economic problems. Too many churches, whether small or large, are ill-equipped to respond to such problems. Indeed, the problems can be overwhelming. Yet, if the church would adopt cooperative, educational programs, real progress in empowering people to achieve is possible.

In fact, I strongly believe that only the church can impact the plight of the poor in a meaningful way. Government programs have a place, but they are only Band-Aids, addressing a specific physical need of some sort. The spiritual domain is neglected, and this leads to a repeating scenario: The soup kitchen or clothing bank continues to struggle because the number of people who are in need seldom decreases. In my experience, the numbers increase. Empowering these people who are, in the words of one author, "on the underside of society" is the goal of urban church education. Give a person a fish and you feed them for a day, but teach a person to fish and they feed themselves for a lifetime.

In the survey I conducted in 1996, I asked, "How would you describe empowering education?" Pastors gave such responses as "to inspire students to apply the knowledge acquired" or "providing the student with the tools and faith to succeed in life" or "skills necessary for employment" or "to motivate students to achieve and succeed." These responses center on the theme of achievement. I believe the body of Christ found in the local church can empower the poor, the oppressed, and the disenfranchised to rise above their situation and become contributing members of society.

Urban church education works with the public school to supplement its task for poor and working-class families. Jonathan Kozol claims in his book *Savage Inequalities* that the urban public schools are more likely to be underfunded than their suburban counterparts, thus leading to inferior education. I believe that Kozol's claims and other evidence show that a class divide in public education is being created. Public schools are attempting to respond to the poor job they are doing by offering schools for the "haves" and schools for the "have-nots." For example, magnet schools and charter schools separate students this way. And of course, the private schools are famous for separating the wealthy from the poor. This division hurts the poor and working classes because their children receive an inferior education.

So another question for pastors in the survey was whether they believed that "the urban church has a responsibility to supplement the education children and youth receive from the public school." Ninety-four percent responded "yes." Moreover, asked if they had any programs at their church to address the need, 88 percent of the pastors responded that they did. When asked to describe these programs, this was the response: 30 percent, after school; 15 percent, adult training school; 39 percent, GED classes; and 45 percent, tutoring classes.

A local church that encourages and inspires its parishioners to achieve will set people free through empowering programs—programs that give a hand up, not just a handout. Urban church education is really about the liberation of people from physical, spiritual, and mental oppression. Joseph Durham says, "Having done battle with myriads of problems during the week, the average adult wants some message of hope and comfort."[1] Ultimately, urban church education offers such a message.

With this book I have sought to provide a resource for the person who has little or no training in Christian education, but has been charged with the responsibility of coordinating the

Sunday school or other special programs for children or young adults. Among the churches included in my survey, 43 percent of the people who directed their educational programs had either no training or only practical experience; only 21 percent had a degree in education.

Church educational programs must go beyond simply imparting information if they are to achieve the goal of transformation. The urban church must reestablish its historic role as the educational center of the black community. I believe the church can do that and can once again assert its relevance by embracing an empowering philosophy in its programs. I have endeavored to give some definition to what an empowering approach would look like within the urban setting. It is important to have a coherent philosophy of education with realistic goals and not just to go along with the enthusiasm that is easily engendered.

I know from my own experience that it is often easiest for empowerment to begin at the Sunday school level. Then other programs, like those described in the case studies, can be explored.

The survey showed that many churches already have some sort of empowering educational program. For example, the Reverend Dr. Ernestine C. Reems of the Center of Hope Community Church in Oakland, California, indicated that the church sponsored an after-school program offering tutoring assistance and computer learning for school-aged neighborhood children and teenagers. The Reverend Boyce Jordan Jr., pastor of Christian Hope Missionary Baptist Church in Philadelphia, Pennsylvania, described a peer counseling program for young adults called Cultural Enrichment Through Education (Project CEE). These are only two examples. But the message is clear: Many churches are establishing programs that empower. The approach is shifting from giving the poor and oppressed a handout to giving them a hand up.

I have selected case studies that have this empowering focus, a solid philosophy, and obtainable goals. I chose not to include

programs that seemed simply to offer good ideas that the organizers had not yet worked through.

My experiences at Evangel Temple and elsewhere and the
writing of this book have persuaded me all the more that
empowerment is a major ministry that the church of Jesus
Christ—especially the urban church—should embrace. Empowerment seeks to motivate people to better their situation. Hence,
the church in urban areas can once again become relevant by
providing a hand-up ministry.

Questions for Discussion

1. In your own words summarize the author's reflections
   on urban church education.
2. List at least five key ideas you have learned from this
   book.
3. The author says that "the urban church must reestablish its historic role as the educational center of the
   black community." Do you agree? Why or why not?
4. What type of educational programs would you recommend for your local church to empower people to
   achieve?

Teaching Black Adults in the Sunday School

Joseph T. Durham*

Introduction

I have attended Sunday school for as long as I can remember. In fact, my earliest memories are those of sitting in what was known as the "card" class and hearing the teacher talk about St. Paul's call to go to some far-off land called Macedonia. Later on I became a Sunday school teacher myself. I have taught both high school students and adults. I hope that the suggestions made here will be helpful to those who work with African American adults in Sunday school today.

Have you ever gone to an adult Bible class on Sunday, eager to learn, only to have the teacher begin by saying, "Does any one have anything to say on the lesson?" You came to hear what the *teacher* had to say on the lesson.

Or, have you gone to the adult class and had the teacher "preach" the lesson instead of teaching the lesson? Teachers should know that the Sunday school is a teaching station, not a preaching station.

---

*Used by permission. Joseph T. Durham (Ed.D., Columbia University) is a leading layman of the United Holy Church of America, Inc., the oldest African American Pentecostal church body in the United States. A Sunday school teacher for many years, he is president emeritus of the Community College of Baltimore and currently professor of education at Morgan State University in Baltimore.

How can we successfully reach black adults in Sunday school?

While it is true that most learners learn the same way, we cannot teach adults the same way we teach children. With children we dramatize, role-play, use flash cards, have cut-outs, build dioramas, and engage in a multiplicity of activities. All learners should be active, but for adults the action should be different.

A Week Ends, A Week Begins

The black adult who comes to our Sunday school class has usually come through a week full of responsibility and perhaps not a little trial. In fact, when the black adult enters the class on Sunday, he/she presents a challenge to the teacher, who must compete with stress and uneasiness that has been caused by being battered with health problems, financial problems, employment problems, and family problems. Having done battle with myriads of problems during the week, the average adult wants some message of hope and comfort. He or she wants the "blessed assurance" that God is in His heaven, and while all may not be right with the world (as Robert Browning put it), at least the adult Christian wants to have his faith lifted. He/she has the right to expect that after fighting traffic six days and working forty hours, they will receive instruction to enable them to carry on for another week.

The challenge for the teacher of black adults is to find a point of relevance in the lesson to the situation and circumstances of the learners. To do this, the teacher must know the students.

He/she must know something about their lives, their problems, their aspirations, and their goals. With this knowledge in mind, the teacher must find ways to tie the lessons to the concerns of the class members. A lesson that is not made relevant will not be very useful to hurried and harried adults.

How, for example, can we make lesson material from Zephaniah and Habakkuk relevant to black adults in the 1990s?

One way is to establish parallels. These minor prophets lived in a day among Old Testament men and women who were clearly black. In the Old Testament, Moses' wife was a woman of color. Again, in the Old Testament, Jeremiah's life was saved by an Ethiopian (Jeremiah 38:7–13). In the New Testament, Philip the Evangelist preached near Gaza to an Ethiopian high government official (Acts 8:29–39). Also, the New Testament church clearly had blacks who held prominent places in the church at Antioch (Acts 13:1).

The alert teacher will never miss the opportunity, where justified, to cite the instances where a black presence in the ancient world existed. Such citations will help the black adult to have a keener appreciation of the biblical record and to realize the truth of St. Peter's word that "God is no respecter of persons." In racist America, where eleven o'clock on Sunday morning is still the most racially segregated hour in America, such a realization is a powerful boost to black self-esteem.

Adults do not want to be preached to in Sunday school. This is why ministers probably should not be assigned as teachers in the adult Bible class. (Historically, the Sunday school has been a laymen's organization.) Adults have problems, questions, and concerns that need to be addressed during the course of a lesson. In short, they need and want to dialogue, and abundant opportunities for dialogue and discussion will be provided by a good teacher of adults.

Discussions should be focused; they should not be rambling; they should end with some conclusion (perhaps tentative) or with questions for further discussion.

There are times in a dynamic lesson when spontaneous discussions arise; however, discussions should, in the main, be planned. This is why the teacher of adults comes to class with prepared discussion questions and knows when they will be used. Some lesson quarterlies contain discussion questions that may be helpful, but those prepared by a teacher with a specific group of class members in mind are better.

Turning the Sunday school lesson into a reading lesson is a sure-fire way to turn most black adults off. This is particularly true in the case of senior citizens who may not be the most skillful readers. Calling on them to read aloud the lesson text can be a source of embarrassment. It is doubtful that reading the lesson text or commentary serves any useful purpose. Students should be encouraged to read the entire lesson before coming to class, thus leaving adequate time for discussion and explanation.

In order to be successful, the teacher should have adequately thought through how he will begin the lesson, how to proceed, and how to end the lesson. Many teachers write out their plans; others have clearly outlined their plans in their minds. While the writer prefers a written plan, mental plans are acceptable. The point is that successful lessons are planned carefully.

One thing that a conscientious teacher plans for is how to summarize and end the lesson. Lessons should not just end abruptly. It has been suggested that one-third of the lesson time should be devoted to ending the lesson and the summary.

Various means may be used to wrap up the lesson. A general method is to have students react to a series of open-ended statements such as these:

1. One thing I can believe is _____.
2. One thing I am encouraged to do is _____.
3. One thing that this passage teaches about relationships is _____.
4. The Good News I find in this passage which meets one of my needs is _____.

These open-ended statements can be used with almost any lesson. Teachers should constantly search for other ways to summarize and end their lesson presentations.

It is reported that the parishioners of one black middle-class congregation complained to their pastor that an elderly lady invariably slept each Sunday morning during service. (We are not told whether she snored or not!) Repeatedly, the parishioners complained to the pastor. Finally, one day the pastor answered them by saying that the lady's sleeping did not bother him at all. "If," he said, "in the midst of all of her trials and tribulations, the church provided her a place of rest for an hour or so each Sunday morning, that is all right with me."

The story may be apocryphal, but it contains a kernel of truth. The black church serves a number of purposes. Historically, it has served as our school, our concert hall, our lecture platform, and a forum for community issues. In the case of the lady in the story, it has served as a place away from the cares of a mean and hostile world for a season.

The same case can be made for the church school for the black adult learner. The Bible church school for the black adult serves a special need. What do black adults look for in their church school classes? In a word, they look for a word from the Scripture that will help make sense of the world and assist them to grow into the measure of the fullest stature in Christ.

This is a tall order. But if the teacher of black adults does not help his students to achieve Christian growth, he is missing the mark. Various methods and procedures are available to the teacher of adults. Some are presented here. I make no brief that these are foolproof, but they are drawn from my experience in teaching black adults in Sunday schools of the United Holy Church of America. I present examples under the following three headings:

A. Getting students to express their feelings.

B. Getting students to think about a problem.

C. Getting students to do more than sit and listen.

Many adult learners are reluctant to express their feelings and/or opinions in public. On the other hand, there are some more vocal ones who will monopolize the class unless they are restrained.

To draw out the reluctant ones, the presentation of a set of preconceived situations with instructions to write down a thought or two about it can help some students to "open up" in class. The following exercise has been used with success.

Exercise 1

Identifying Your Feelings

What are your true feelings about the poor and the oppressed? Below are some statements. Try to evaluate how you feel about them by circling the letter of the statement that comes closest to how you feel.

> A. I feel furious.
> B. I have no feelings about this.
> C. I feel helpless.
> D. I feel they got what they deserved.

After you evaluate each of the statements, write a short sentence giving the reason for your evaluation.

A B C D   1. A 15-year-old black is convicted of armed robbery and rape after a white woman selected his picture from a "Rogues Gallery."

Reason _____

A B C D   2. A welfare mother goes to jail for cheating the state government of $10,000 over a three-year period by falsifying records and affidavits.

Reason _____

A B C D   3. A daily metropolitan newspaper reports that many elderly couples in the United States and Canada can only afford dog food as the major part of their diet.

Reason _____

A B C D   4. A professional man whose salary is over $40,000 per year complains that he cannot afford to send his daughter to college, and because of his income, she cannot qualify for student financial assistance from the government.

Reason _____

A B C D   5. In a suburb, white men attacked a school bus and poured oil on black and Puerto Rican students being transported to a white school.

Reason _____

When the students have reacted to these instances, a discussion follows. The teacher can use their answers to relate to certain biblical principles and ethical teachings.

Exercise 2

Thinking about a Problem

Adults encounter problems on a twenty-four-hour basis. They are used to solving problems in the secular arena. Why not tap these developed skills and assist the adults to apply problem-solving skills to situations that have religious implications or lead them to apply religious principles. The following "problem" situations have provoked vigorous discussions in some classes I have taught.

Problem 1

First Pentecostal Church has a large, active youth group headed by Brother Joe, who serves as youth pastor. Brother Joe is a college graduate who became acquainted with the black celebration of Kwanza, which is celebrated at Christmas time. Kwanza was originated as a celebration to unify blacks and make them appreciate their African heritage.

Kwanza is celebrated for a period of approximately a week and emphasizes such concepts as brotherhood, love, industry, faith, and purity. For a Kwanza observance, a group gathers around a candle, and another is lit each evening until eight candles are lit. The group shares and exchanges small gifts and eats fruits and nuts.

Brother Joe believes that the young peoples group should have a Kwanza celebration along with the regular Christmas celebration. The senior pastor has objected. What should the young people and Brother Joe do?

Problem 2

John Bright is a deacon in First Church. By trade, he is a carpenter whose union hall is located over a bar in the downtown section of the city. The bar and the union hall share a common entrance. Deacon Bright is unemployed at the moment. If he wants to work, he must go to the union hall and read the bulletin board. The problem is that Deacon Bright will be seen going into the same entrance that leads to the bar. John has so far refused to look for work at the union hall because he is afraid his position as a deacon in the church will be compromised if he is seen entering a building in which a bar is also located.

Questions:

    a. What should Deacon Bright do?
    b. If you were in this situation, what would you do?
    c. Do you know anyone who has been in a similar situation? What did that person do?

Exercise 3

Don't Just Sit and Listen

Perhaps the dear lady who slept in church on Sunday morning might not have done so if she had been engaged in some activity. Adult education focuses on the fact that learners are a rich resource for learning and their contributions should be tapped during each lesson session. The following exercise caused learners to sit up and participate.

Where Should a Christian Be Seen?

Yes	No	Never	(Check)
❏	❏	❏	1. At the beach in swimwear
❏	❏	❏	2. At a movie theater
❏	❏	❏	3. At a basketball game at the local arena
❏	❏	❏	4. At a Redskins game on a Sunday afternoon
❏	❏	❏	5. At the office Christmas party
❏	❏	❏	6. At the neighborhood summer block festival
❏	❏	❏	7. At a local restaurant that has an ABC license
❏	❏	❏	8. At a concert of the group "Take Six"
❏	❏	❏	9. At a Muslim religious service

Principles Involved

_____

_____

These examples may suggest others for the conscientious teacher. Jesus, the Master Teacher of adults, certainly employed numerous educational methods in His ministry. He lectured, asked questions, gave assignments, required reports, led His disciples in various projects, and made use of the dramatic method quite a bit in His teaching, in either a formal or an informal manner.

The successful teacher of adults is constantly in search of ways and means to appeal to his students.

A few suggestions have been made that may prove helpful. It has been said that the good teacher should pray himself hot, read himself full, and think himself empty.

Urban Church Education Survey

In conducting this survey in 1996, I mailed a total of 32 questionnaires to predominantly black churches. The churches that received surveys were those for whom I had ministered in the past or whose personnel I met at a ministers' conference. Of the 32 surveys mailed out, I received 16 back, which represented 50 percent. The following eight states were represented in this survey: Virginia, New Jersey, North Carolina, Pennsylvania, New York, Georgia, California, and Maryland. Finally, there were 13 cities represented in the survey: Newport News, VA; Franklin, VA; Washington, DC; Trenton, NJ; Greensboro, NC; Norristown and Pittsburgh, PA; Rochester, Far Rockaway, and The Bronx, NY; Atlanta, GA; Oakland, CA; and Baltimore, MD.

The attached survey will greatly assist me in my research on the topic of "Urban Religious Education." Thank you for taking the time to complete it.

Please complete the following information before beginning:

Name/Title_____ Phone _____

Name of Church_____

Address _____

City _____ Zip _____

Approx. Attendance_____

Affiliation (If Applicable)_____

Type of Church (Facilities)   ____ Store Front
                              ____ Traditional Bldg.
                              ____ Renting Facilities
Location of Church   ____ Inner City
                              ____ Rural/Suburban
                              ____ Suburban
                              ____ Urban (on Fringe of City)
Size of Membership   ____* Attendance on Sunday a.m.
                              ____ Adults (Over 18) Attending
                              ____ Youth (12-18) Attending
                              ____ Children (0-12) Attending

*The congregational sizes varied in the following manner.

Size	Respondents
150–200	3
300–475	4
500–700	3
1000–2000	5
3300–	1

1. List in order of importance (1–4) what you consider to be the most important tasks of the urban church today.

—— Evangelism   —— Feeding the poor
—— Social justice   —— Education

2. From your perspective, does the urban church have a responsibility to supplement the education children and youth receive from the public schools?

—— Yes   —— No

Explain your response.

_____

_____

_____

3. Does your church offer any programs or ministry to help children and youth succeed in public schools?

—— Yes   —— No

If so, list a few of them.

_____

_____

_____

4. In your opinion, does Christian instruction only occur formally in Sunday school or education classes within the church?

—— Yes   —— No

Mention any informal ways it may occur.

_____

_____

_____

_____

5. How is your church addressing the need for Christian instruction in your neighborhood?
   ____ After school program ____ Adult training school
   ____ GED classes   ____ Tutoring program
   ____ List any other

6. Should the major thrust of Christian instruction, particularly for the urban context, be informal (impartation of knowledge) or empowering (ability to perform)?
   ____ Informational   ____ Empowering

7. Which of the following terms do you think best describes empowering education? (Choose one)

   ____ Inspire students to learn and to do something with the knowledge obtained

   ____ Providing the student with tools and faith to succeed in life

   ____ Teaching others to reach others

   ____ Lifts the student's horizons to high heights

   ____ Skills necessary for employment

   ____ Become a disciple

   ____ Motivate students to achieve

8. What area(s)of training would be beneficial to teachers in your Christian education department?
   ____ How to teach the Scriptures
   ____ Structure and organization
   ____ Teaching methods
   ____ How to get students to apply the lesson
   ____ Team teaching.
   List any others:

   _____

   _____

9. Do you have a person(s) who specifically coordinates your Christian education department?

—— Yes   —— No

10. What are the qualifications of that person(s)?

—— Practical experience   —— School teacher
—— No training   —— Other

11. How would you describe your approach or philosophy of Christian education? In other words, how does your church accomplish the task of "teaching" as commanded by Christ in Matthew 28:20?

_____

_____

_____

12. How many male teachers are involved in your education ministry?

_____

_____

_____

13. In your opinion, what is the most effective area(s) of ministry to empower African American males?

—— Male only class   —— Self-esteem workshops
—— Job skills   —— Mentoring program
—— Fatherhood classes   —— Counseling service

14. In the same vein as the above, what about African American females?

—— Female only class   —— Self-esteem workshops
—— Job skills   —— Mentoring program
—— Motherhood classes   —— Crisis counseling service

A City-Dweller's Prayer

Ernest T. Campbell

O God of every time and place,
Prevail among us too;
Within the city that we love,
its promise to renew.
Our people move with downcast eye,
tight, sullen and afraid;
Surprise us with Thy joy divine
for we would be remade.

O Thou whose will we can resist,
but cannot overcome,
Forgive our harsh and strident ways,
the harm that we have done.
Like Babel's builders long ago
we raise our lofty towers,
And like them, too, our words divide,
and pride lays waste our powers.

Behind the masks that we maintain
to shut our sadness in,
There lurks the hope, however dim,
to live once more as men.
Let wrong embolden us to fight,
and need excite our care;
If not us, who? If not now, when?
If not here, God, then where?

Our fathers stayed their minds on Thee
  in village, farm and plain;
Help us, their crowded, harried kin,
  no less Thy peace to claim.
Give us to know that Thou dost love
  each soul that Thou has made;
That size does not diminish grace,
  nor concrete hide Thy gaze.

Grant us, O God, who labor here
  within this throbbing maze,
A forward-looking, saving hope
  to galvanize our days.
Let Christ, who loved Jerusalem,
  and wept its sins to mourn,
Make just our laws and pure our hearts.

Amen.

Notes

CHAPTER 2

1. Cornelius Van Til, *Foundations of Christian Education*, ed. Dennis E. Johnson (Phillipsburg, NJ: Presbyterian and Reformed, 1990), 3.
2. Donald B. Rogers, ed. *Urban Church Education* (Birmingham, AL: Religious Education Press, 1989), 12.
3. Ibid., 12.
4. Robert C. Linthicum, *Empowering the Poor* (Monrovia, CA: MARC, 1991), 21.
5. Ibid., 22.
6. Ibid., 23.
7. Roger S. Greenway, ed. *Discipling The City second edition* (Grand Rapids: Baker Book House, 1993), 36.
8. Wayne Robinson, interview with the author, Greensboro, NC, November 1996.
9. Center for Champions brochure, Greensboro, NC, 1996, 1.

CHAPTER 3

1. J. John Palen, *The Urban World*, 4th ed. (New York: McGraw-Hill, 1992), 9.
2. Larry L. Rose and C. Kirk Hadaway, *An Urban World* (Nashville: Broadman Press, 1984), 20–21.
3. Louis Wirth, "Urbanization as a Way of Life," in *Cities and Churches*, ed. Robert Lee (Philadelphia: Westminister Press, 1962), 21–33.
4. Ibid., 21.
5. John Gulick, *The Humanity of Cities* (Boston: Bergin and Garvey, 1989), 6.
6. Roger S. Greenway and Timothy M. Monsma, *Cities: Mission's New Frontier* (Grand Rapids: Baker Book House, 1989), 61.
7. Harvie M. Conn, *A Clarified Vision For Urban Mission* (Grand Rapids: Zondervan, 1987), 65.
8. Harv Oostdyk, *Step One: The Gospel and the Ghetto* (Basking Ridge, NJ: Sonlife International, 1983), 36.

9. David Claerbaut, *Urban Ministry* (Grand Rapids: Zondervan, 1983), 15. See also comments in Rose and Hadaway, *An Urban World*, 20–21.

10. Ibid., 32.

11. Harvie M. Conn, *The American City and the Evangelical Church* (Grand Rapids: Baker Books, 1994), 121–22. Also note his insightful analysis of the rise of poverty, homelessness, and drugs, 124–28. See the excellent article by Ron Wilson, "Momma, When We Goin' Home?" in *World Vision* 33 (April/May 1989), 4–9, in which the author provides statistical analysis of about half a million children growing up homeless in the United States.

12. Gulick, *The Humanity of Cities*, 6.

13. Ann K. Umstead, interview with the author, Greensboro, NC, November 1996.

14. Anita B. Carter, interview by telephone, October 28, 1997.

15. "Getting to Know Your Caregiving Employee," Adult Center for Enrichment, Greensboro, NC, 1996.

CHAPTER 4

1. Bishop John L. Meares was fond of saying that "if the body of Jesus Christ would really be the body of Jesus Christ in the inner city, it could be used by God to transform the inner city into a beautiful garden in the ghetto which would be the envy of every suburban community" (sermon preached at Evangel Temple, Washington, DC, October 1985).

2. Paulo Freire, *Pedagogy of the Oppressed* (New York: Continuum Publications, 1990), 57.

3. Ibid., 58.

4. *The Spirit-Filled Life Bible*, ed. Jack W. Hayford (Nashville: Thomas Nelson, 1991), 1622.

5. Gustavo Gutierréz, *A Theology of Liberation* (Maryknoll, NY: Orbis Books, 1990).

6. James Cone, *Black Theology and Black Power* (New York: Seabury Press, 1969).

7. J. Deotis Roberts, *Liberation and Reconciliation: A Black Theology* (Philadelphia: Westminster Press, 1971). Read page 48 for a summary of his theology.

8. Carl F. Ellis Jr., *Beyond Liberation* (Downers Grove, IL: InterVarsity Press, 1983), 175.

9. William H. Cook, *Success, Motivation, and the Scriptures* (Nashville: Broadman Press, 1974), 19.

10. Ibid., 44.
11. Francis Frangipane, *The House of the Lord* (Lake Mary, FL: Creation House, 1991), 11.
12. Ibid.
13. Mrs. Myrtle Lawson, interview with the author, at Cana Baptist Church, Washington, DC, March 11, 1998.

CHAPTER 5
1. I am deeply grateful for the dialogue regarding Christian education I have had over the years with Dr. Corinthia Boone, my predecessor at Evangel Temple.
2. Mount Zion Baptist Church has four thousand members, and the Reverend George Brooks is the senior pastor.
3. The Reverend Kevin Lee, interview with the author, Greensboro, NC, November 13, 1996.

CHAPTER 6
1. The Reverend Carl Manuel Jr., interview with the author, Greensboro, NC, November 1996.

CHAPTER 7
1. Carter G. Woodson. *The Mis-Education of the Negro* (Trenton, NJ: Africa World Press, Inc., 1990, 1933 reprint), xiii.
2. See the following works that document the appalling conditions of city schools in America; in each case, the authors point out the fact that city schools receive less funding than suburban schools: Jonathan Kozol, *Savage Inequalities: Children in America's Schools* (New York: Crown, 1991); William J. Wilson, *The Truly Disadvantaged: The Inner City, the Underclass and Public Policy* (Chicago: University of Chicago Press, 1987); and S. Bowles and S. Gintis, *Schooling in Capitalist America: Education and the Contradictions of Economic Life* (New York: Basic Books, 1976).
3. Thomas E. Leland, *Developing a Model of Religious Education for Black Southern Baptist Churches* (Ed.D. dissertation from Southern Baptist Theological Seminary, Louisville, KY, 1981), 36.
4. Colleen Birchett, "A History of Religious Education in the Black Church," in *Urban Church Education*, Donald B. Rogers, ed. (Birmingham, AL: Religious Education Press, 1989), 72.

5. Leland, *Developing a Model*, 37.

6. Albert J. Raboteau, *Slave Religion* (New York: Oxford University Press, 1978), 165.

7. Leland, *Developing a Model of Religious Education*, 41.

8. Ibid., 40.

9. Ibid., 48.

10. James O. Buswell III, *Slavery, Segregation, and Scripture* (Grand Rapids: Eerdmans, 1964), 28–29.

11. E. Dorian Gadsden, *Progress against the Tide* (New York: Vantage Press, 1989). See his discussion of the slaves codes of Virginia from 1662 to 1680 on pages 6–9.

12. Buswell, *Slavery, Segregation, and Scripture*. See his cogent presentation of the biblical arguments for slavery in chapter 1, "Scriptural Justification for Slavery," 12–18.

13. E. Franklin Frazier, *The Negro Church in America* (New York: Schocken Books, 1964), 46.

14. C. Eric Lincoln and Lawrence H. Mamiya, *The Black Church in the African American Experience* (Durham, NC: Duke University Press, 1990), 8.

15. Joseph T. Durham, "Teaching Black Adults in Sunday School" unpublished paper, 1993. Dr. Durham gave me a copy of this paper in 1997, and he has granted me permission to include it as an appendix in this book.

16. Quoted in Leland, *Developing a Model of Religious Education*. For a thorough study of the educational programs for former slaves during the Reconstruction era, see Carter G. Woodson, *The History of the Negro Church*, 3d ed. (Washington, DC: Associated Publishers, 1972), 51.

17. Gadsden, *Progress against the Tide*, 42.

18. Leland, *Developing a Model of Religious Education*, 52.

19. Ibid., 53.

20. James D. Anderson, *The Education of Blacks in the South, 1860–1935* (Chapel Hill, NC: University of North Carolina Press, 1988), 4.

21. Ibid., 5.

22. Ibid., 173.

23. Ibid., 171.

24. Interview with Bishop Alfred Owens Jr. on August 2, 2001.

CHAPTER 8

1. Harry Blamires, *The Christian Mind* (Ann Arbor, MI: Servant Books, 1963), 3.

2. James D. Cunningham and Anthony C. Fortosis, *Education in Christian Schools* (Whittier, CA: Association of Christian Schools International, 1987), 16–17.

3. James Hitchcock, *What Is Secular Humanism?* (Ann Arbor, MI: Servant Books, 1982), 10–11.

4. Cunningham and Fortosis, *Education in Christian Schools,* 19.

5. R. C. Sproul, *Life Views: Understanding Ideas That Shape Society Today* (Old Tappan, NJ: Fleming H. Revell, 1986), 84–85.

6. Ibid., 43.

7. Cunningham, *Education in Christian Schools,* 19.

8. Dennis Peacocke, *Winning the Battle for the Minds of Men* (Santa Rosa, CA: Alive and Free, 1987), xiii.

9. Robert W. Pazmiño, *Fundamental Issues in Christian Education* (Grand Rapids: Baker Book House, 1988), 75–76.

10. Ibid., 76.

11. See the following Scripture references: Matthew 6:25–34; Luke 12:22–34; Philippians 4:6; 1 Peter 5:7.

12. Blamires, *The Christian Mind,* 43.

13. Jack Layman, "Histories of Educational Philosophies," in *Philosophy of Christian Education,* ed. Paul E. Kienel (Colorado Springs: Association of Christian Schools International, 1995), 53.

14. Ibid., 58.

15. Ibid., 65. Also, for some excellent analysis of the roots of Western dualism, see Christian Overman, *Different Windows* (Wheaton, IL: Tyndale House, 1989), and Francis A. Schaeffer, *Escape from Reason* (Downers Grove, IL: InterVarsity Press, 1968).

16. Werner C. Graendorf, ed., *Introduction to Biblical Christian Education* (Chicago: Moody 1981), 16. For other definitions of Christian education, see Roy B. Zuck, *Spiritual Power of Your Teaching,* rev. ed. (Chicago: Moody, 1972), 9; and Norman DeJong, *Education in the Truth* (Nutley, NJ: Presbyterian and Reformed, 1974), 118.

17. K. Patricia Cross, *Adult Learners* (San Francisco: Jossey-Bass Publishers, 1981), 222.

18. Joseph T. Durham, "Teaching Black Adults in Sunday School" (unpublished paper, 1993), 1.

CONCLUSION

1. Joseph T. Durham, "Teaching Black Adults in Sunday School" (unpublished paper, 1993).

Annotated Bibliography

African-American Studies

Feagin, Joe E. "The Continuing Significance of Race: Anti Black Discrimination in Public Places." *American Sociological Review* 56 (February 1991): 101–16.

A look at the problematic question of racism in public accommodations for middle-class blacks. Feagin also explores how middle-class blacks cope with the other forms of racism manifested during the 1990s. He interviewed 37 middle-class blacks from several large urban centers and discussed with them specific citations of racial discrimination. He concludes that racism is still a pervasive part of American society.

Hacker, Andrew. *Two Nations.* New York: Charles Scribner's Sons, 1992.

A provocative critique of current race relations between blacks and whites. The author's premise is that the pervasive attitude of black inferiority among whites has not disappeared in spite of civil rights legislation and the tremendous gains by black people. Hacker examines all aspects of black/white choices from education to neighborhoods and employment to determine the pervasiveness racism is in America. He concludes that blacks and whites in essence comprise two nations.

Samkange, Stanlake. *African Saga.* Nashville: Abingdon Press, 1971.

A brief introduction to African history. Despite the author's acceptance of an evolutionary origin of mankind, the book has helpful data concerning the history of black people in Africa.

Steele, Shelby. *The Content of Our Character.* New York: St. Martin's Press, 1990.

A book whose title is derived from a phrase in the famous "I Have a Dream" speech by Dr. Martin Luther King Jr. Steele contends that black people must stop seeing themselves from a victim's mindset and consequently overcome white racist society by individual achievement. With candid and persuasive arguments he shows how both blacks and whites have been trapped into seeing color before character. Steele is concerned with motivating black people to move beyond racism to individual achievement.

West, Cornel. *Race Matters*. Boston: Beacon Press, 1993.

An analysis of race relations addressed through essays such as "The Crisis of Black Leadership," "Nihilism in Black America," and "Black-Jewish Relations." West's critique reaches beyond the traditional liberal-conservation rhetoric to the heart of the matter. He provides a transformative voice that needs to be heard because the nation is confronted with racial matters.

Apologetics

Schaeffer, Francis A. *The God Who is There*. Downers Grove, IL: InterVarsity Press, 1968.

An exploration of the idea that only historic Christianity can aptly respond to man's quest for truth. Schaeffer repudiates secularism and liberal theology and notes that historic Christianity supplies the logical answers to critical questions about man's nature and the construction of the real world in which we live.

_____. *He Is There and He Is Not Silent*. Wheaton, IL: Tyndale House, 1972.

A case for the need for a contemporary Christian presentation of metaphysics (the study of ultimate reality) and epistemology (the study of knowledge). The author contends that Christianity provides a rational response to the various realities found in mankind's daily existence and moral/ethical dilemma. This book is an excellent resource for addressing an unbelieving and nonrational world with a Christian response.

Black History

Bennett, Lerone, Jr. *Before the Mayflower*. 5th edition. Chicago: Johnson Publisher, 1982.

A classic textbook on the history of black people in America from 1619 to 1981. Bennett espouses that black people have been a part of American history since its beginnings.

Dubois, W. E. B. *The Soul of Black Folk.* New York: Fawcett, 1961.

A look at the problem of racism in America, written as a wonderfully textured portrait of dispossessed people in search of themselves in a hostile environment. Dubois explores the struggle of black people for freedom and dignity.

Gadsden, Dorian E. *Progress against the Tide.* New York: Vantage Press, 1989.

A well-researched book that documents the progress of African-Americans in the United States against racism and oppression. Gadsden holds that African-Americans have made significant progress, though that progress has come slowly and at great cost.

Haley, Alex. *The Autobiography of Malcolm X.* New York: Ballantine Books, 1992.

A classic in autobiographical genre. This is the story of a man who was a hoodlum, drug user, and burglar and then, through religious conversion to Islam, became a leading voice in the struggle for justice. Malcolm X best articulated the anger of black people in their struggle for freedom during the early 1960s.

Harding, Vincent. "The Acts of God and the Children of Africa." *New Roads to Faith* (September 1972): 3–7.

Based on the conviction that God is known and encountered within the concrete events of history, an exploration of black people's struggle for freedom in America as a remarkable parallel to the liberation of the Hebrew people from Egypt. Harding suggests that the black struggle for freedom is as much an act of God as the liberation of the Hebrews. He further states that the process of instructing black people is incomplete without introducing them to the struggle for freedom, justice, and dignity in America.

King, Martin Luther, Jr. *The Trumpet of Conscience.* San Francisco: Harper & Row, 1967.

A look at the entrenched nature of injustice and evil from a global perspective. King criticizes American involvement in the Vietnam

War and articulates that a massive movement of oppressed people must be organized to combat structures and the elite in power.

_____. *Why We Can't Wait*. New York: Signet, 1964.

An exploration of the reasons why black people could no longer wait for their civil rights. King traces the story of black people's struggle for freedom even during the time of slavery. He also looks at the abysmal failure of the federal government and the courts in ushering in freedom and justice for black people. This book also contains as one of its chapters Dr. King's famous "Letter From Birmingham Jail."

Black Theological Studies

Carter, Stephen L. *The Culture of Disbelief*. New York: Basic Books, 1993.

The view that America is the most religious nation in the Western world, yet many political leaders and opinion makers have come to view any religious element in public discourse as a tool of the Right for reshaping American society. In our sensible zeal to keep religion from dominating our politics, Carter argues, we have constructed political and legal cultures that force the religiously devout to act as if their faith doesn't really matter. He explains how we can preserve the vital separation of church and state while embracing rather than trivializing the faith of millions of citizens or treating religious believers with disdain.

Cone, James H. *A Black Theology of Liberation*. Maryknoll, NY: Orbis Books, 1986.

A scathing indictment of white theology and society that also offers a radical reappraisal of Christianity through the pained and angry eyes of an oppressed black community. Cone's theme is liberation as the key to understanding Christianity from a black perspective.

_____. *God of the Oppressed*. San Francisco: Harper & Row, 1975.

A look at the themes of suffering and liberation of black people in the struggle for justice. Cone examines the norms and sources of black theology in relation to the black experience and belief in Jesus Christ. His black theology views Jesus Christ for today as the liberator of the oppressed.

_____. "The Story Context of Black Theology." *Theology Today* 32 (July 1975): 144–50.

An excellent comparison of white theology and black theology by a leading black theologian. Cone holds that the difference is black theology's centeredness in the theme of liberation. He also notes that while liberation is the content of black theology, story-telling is the method by which the content is delivered.

Dunston, Bishop Alfred G. *The Black Man in the Old Testament and Its World.* Philadelphia: Dorrance, 1974.

Research and analysis of biblical texts in which blacks cross the pages of the Old Testament.

Ellis, Carl, Jr. *Beyond Liberation.* Downers Grove, IL: InterVarsity Press, 1983.

An account of the development of black consciousness from slavery to the present. Ellis explores various themes, such as freedom and spirituals, and various figures, such as Malcolm X and Martin Luther King Jr., to show how God's grace was evident in the triumphs and defeats of black people in their journey toward freedom. Ellis's premise is that black people need to move beyond political liberation to spiritual liberation by God's grace.

Evans, James H., Jr. *We Have Been Believers.* Minneapolis: Fortress Press, 1992.

A cogent outline of the scope and richness of African-American religious belief. Evans provides a first-class systematic theology for African-Americans. He seeks to overcome the chasm between church practice and theological reflection.

Hicks, H. Beecher, Jr. *Images of the Black Preacher.* Valley Forge, PA: Judson Press, 1978.

An analysis of both the negative and positive contemporary images of the black preacher. Hicks sees urban black ministers as having a difficult job as they are called upon to heal broken spirits and give meaning to the life of an oppressed people.

Lincoln, Eric C., and Lawrence H. Mamiya. *The Black Church in African American Experience.* Durham, NC: Duke University Press, 1990.

A comprehensive study of the black church from a historical and sociological perspective.

Mitchell, Henry H. *Black Preaching.* Nashville: Abingdon Press, 1990.

A persuasive demonstration that black culture and preaching style are vital for the empowerment of black congregations and have much to offer to the preaching method of all preachers. By focusing on the use of story telling, imagination, and a style of preaching rooted in black culture, the author spotlights effective techniques for lively preaching.

Paris, Peter J. *The Social Teaching of the Black Churches.* Philadelphia: Fortress, Press, 1985.

A constructive interpretation of the moral and political dimensions of the black church in America. The fundamental values of the black church are rooted in what the author calls "the black Christian tradition." Paris contends that the equality of all humanity before God is basic to the black church and that equality, justices, and freedom are part of the black Christian tradition.

Roberts, J. Deotis. *Liberation and Reconciliation: A Black Theology.* Philadelphia: Westminster Press, 1971.

An appeal based on the author's contention that black theologians are good at saying what they are against and that it is time for them to state what they are for. Roberts then articulates a black theology that sees the importance of liberation but also sees reconciliation as consistent with historic Christianity. Roberts's primary concern is with theological ethics.

Skinner, Tom. *How Black Is the Gospel?* New York: Trumpet Books, 1976.

A case for the relevance of the gospel of Jesus Christ for black people in a white racist society. Skinner contends that a relevant gospel liberates black people to struggle against injustice and racism. The book is a critique of white evangelical theology that doesn't see the relevance of the black struggle for freedom.

Washington, Joseph R. *Black Religion*. Boston: Beacon Press, 1964.

A study of the religion of black people in the United States.

Wimberly, Edward P. *African American Pastoral Care*. Nashville: Abingdon Press, 1991.

How pastors and counselors can care for African Americans by using a narrative method. Wimberly demonstrates how to link personal stories to the heart language of Bible stories so that counselors can use God's unfolding drama to bring healing and reconciliation to human lives. He suggests several narrative counseling techniques, including unfolding, linking, thickening, and twisting. In addition, he discusses the relationship of narrative counseling techniques to narrative aspects of preaching and worship.

Christian Education

Barron, Robert. *Understanding People*. Wheaton, IL: Evangelical Training Association, 1989.

A discussion of the various stages of human development from childhood through adolescence and adulthood and some practical advice for ministering to each stage.

Berkhof, Louis, and Cornelius Van Til. *Foundations of Christian Education*, ed. Dennis E. Johnson. Phillipsburg, NJ: Presbyterian and Reformed, 1990.

A biblical and theological rationale for Christian education. Parents place their children in Christian schools for various reasons, such as to escape the evils of public schools. The authors contend that the purpose for the Christian school is not escape, but a means of counteracting the source of the infection that has polluted the education enterprise from within. They therefore see Christian schools as a corrective to non-Christian education.

Brueggeman, Walter, editor. *The Creative Word*. Philadelphia: Fortress Press, 1982.

A study of the various genres of the Old Testament and how Christian education would benefit from the Hebrew tradition. By exploring the traditions of Torah, Wisdom, and the Prophets, the authors suggest that Christian instruction must take into account all aspects of these traditions as a kind of synthesis.

Crockett, Joseph V. *Teaching Scripture from an African-American Perspective*. Nashville: Discipleship Resources, 1989.

The view that African-Americans teach Scripture from a specific perspective grounded in cultural, social, and communal history. Crockett describes four distinct yet related teaching strategies: story, exile, sanctuary, and exodus. Each strategy emphasizes a different facet in the lens of African-American interpretation, biblical content, personal experience, communal tradition, and social analysis and includes an outline of specific steps for teaching.

Cummings, David B., editor. *The Purpose of a Christian School*. Phillipsburg, N.J.: Presbyterian and Reformed, 1979.

A general introduction to the purpose of Christian schools. Each contributor believes the uniqueness of the Christian school is that it seeks to glorify God and train students to be conformed to Jesus Christ. Hence, the Christian school is Christ-centered and not man-centered.

Cunningham, James D., and Anthony C. Fortosis. *Education in Christian Schools*. Whittier, CA: Association of Christian Schools International, 1987.

An excellent book on the proper philosophical base for establishing a Christian school. The authors critically interact with numerous philosophies and demonstrate the superior soundness of Christianity. They suggest that secular and Christian philosophies cannot coexist. One will prevail, and the one that does will control the hearts and minds of American children. The book discusses how American culture and morality have become unraveled and how parents can protect their children at risk.

Gaebelein, Frank E. *The Pattern of God's Truth*. Whittier, CA: Association of Christian Schools International, 1968.

A case for the proposition that at the heart of all thinking about education, whether Christian or secular, lies the problem of integration of knowledge. Gaebelein contends that on this point both Christian and secular education are inadequate, that in many situations integration is seldom given any attention. He discusses how to integrate faith and learning into the educational enterprise.

Gangel, Kenneth O., and Warren S. Benson. *Christian Education: Its History and Philosophy.* Chicago: Moody Press, 1983.

An excellent book that combines both the philosophy and the history of religious education from early Hebrew tradition to contemporary Christianity. Also, the authors focus on cultural/biographical influences, discussing each philosophy in its particular socio-historical setting and giving special attention to significant individuals.

Kennedy, James D. and Jerry Newcombe. *What If Jesus Had Never Been Born?* Nashville: Thomas Nelson, 1994.

An exploration of the contribution the Christian faith has had upon human society. The premise is that the entire structure of human society would be drastically different if Christ had not been born. The authors also provide an apologetic for the Christian faith in response to Nietzsche's scathing critique of it.

LeBar, Lois E. *Education That Is Christian.* Westwood, N.J.: Fleming Revell, 1958.

An answer to the question, Is there a distinctive Christian system of education? The author shows that there is such a system and then defines it. The foundations and orientation of Christian education is very distinctive because Christ is the center and the Scriptures are the guide for life.

Love, James R. "Christian Education and the Black Church." *Urban Mission* 10, no. 1 (September 1992): 37–44.

A study of the question of Christian education in the urban context. Love asks, What can the black church do to reemerge as the educational center in the urban setting? He challenges the black church to become active in the education of black people into the Christian faith.

Miller, Randolph C., editor. "Symposium: Education in the Black Church." *Religious Education* 69, no. 4 (July-August 1974): 403–445.

A symposium focusing on various themes such as black theology and its contribution to religious education, the ethical nature of black education, and the essential role of the black church in educating black people. Among the contributors are Lonzy Edward, Enoch Oglesby, Calvin E. Brice, and Olivia Pearl Stokes.

Palmer, J. Parker. *To Know As We Are Known.* San Francisco: Harper & Row, 1983.

A spirituality of education in which mind and heart work together in the quest for knowledge. The author writes from a contemplative tradition to help the reader gain a more spiritual dimension of education. He convincingly posits that modern education basically amounts to information transmittal. He believes effective teaching creates space so that truth can be obeyed.

Pazmiño, Robert W. *Foundational Issues in Christian Education.* Grand Rapids: Baker, 1988.

An appeal for educators to better deal with current needs and future challenges by critically exploring the various foundations predominant in evangelical thought past and present. To avoid a cultural captivity, Christian education must be rethought by each generation. The author calls evangelical educators both to affirm biblical insights (the essential authority for theory and practice) and to incorporate insights from other disciples (a process that must be subject to the continuing authority of God's Word).

_____. *Principles and Practices of Christian Education.* Grand Rapids: Baker, 1992.

A look at two important principles lying behind all evangelical practice that make Christian educational programs stand out from all others in their nurture of students. First is the need for conversion—personal and corporate transformation that reconnects people to their Creator. Second is the striving for connection—making contact with people as unique individuals who live in a particular society and who need to know more about Scripture.

Reed, James F., and Ronnie Prevost. *A History of Christian Education.* Nashville: Broadman & Holman, 1993.

A wonderful text that recounts the history of Christian education. The authors explore the major figures and theories, both past and present, that have influenced Christian education.

Schockley, Grant S. "Christian Education and the Black Religious Experience." *Ethnicity in the Education of the Church* (June 1987): 29–47.

An excellent article that addresses the need for models of Christian education within the black church. The author sees the task as both theological and practical. In other words, a model of Christian education for the black church must begin with certain theological premises, and from this a practical model must be developed. The church must assume the role of educator and liberator.

_____. "Religious Education and the Black Experience." *The Black Church* 2, no. 1 (September 1973): 91–111.

A look at the important role of the black church in education and affirming the religious experience of black people. He essentially sees the black church as proclaiming a message of liberation and empowerment.

Stokes, Olivia Pearl. "The Educational Role of Black Churches in the '70s and '80s." *New Roads to Faith* (September 1972): 3–27.

An excellent article by a master educator, emphasizing the crucial role black churches will play in education of black people in the 1970s and 1980s. Although the article is dated, Stokes makes several practical suggestions that remain timely to her vision that the black church needs to serve an active role in supplementing public education. For example, she recommends a Saturday school that would tutor black youth in math, science, history, and so on. Stokes views education as a liberation process. She also does a wonderful job of tracing the history of education for black people from slavery to the present.

_____. "The Education of Blacks in the Household of Faith." *Spectrum: Journal of Religious Education* 47, no. 4 (July-August 1971): 5–24.

The lead article in a collection of essays that looks historically at how education was denied to blacks and toward the future in terms of what the church needs to do to empower black people. Other essays address how a Saturday ethnic school would strengthen black youth's understanding of black history. Some essays look at the liberation aspect of Christian education.

Wickett, R. E. Y. *Models of Adult Religious Education and Practice.* Birmingham: Religious Education Press, 1991.

A foundational rationale plus a wide inventory of workable instructional procedures for vitalizing religious education of adults. The author shows in practical ways how adult religious education can most profitably select an instructional model that will optimize its effectiveness with a broad spectrum of learning in different format and informal settings.

Wilhoit, Jim. *Christian Education and the Search for Meaning.* Grand Rapids: Baker, 1986.

The thesis that Christian education has preoccupied itself with the question "How Should We Teach?" and has neglected the question "Why should we teach?" Wilhoit contends that Christian education should teach believers their privileges and responsibilities as "priest" and this should be the road map for their life pilgrimage. The author does an effective job of integrating education, philosophy, theology, and the social science.

Wilhoit, Jim, and LeLand Ryken. *Effective Bible Teaching.* Grand Rapids: Baker, 1988.

Practical instruction on how to teach the Bible. They discuss the process of exegesis, the different biblical genres, and how to locate the biblical idea of a passage.

Christian Family

Dobson, James, and Gary L. Bauer. *Children at Risk.* Dallas: Word, 1990.

A look at the conflicting cultural forces affecting families in American society. On the one side are those who defend family, faith, and traditional values. On the other side are those who aggressively reject any hint of tradition and religion and want a society based on secular principles, the authors contend.

Church Growth

Jackson, Carroll W., editor. *Handbook of Congregational Studies.* Nashville: Abingdon Press, 1986.

A collaborative effort of several researchers who explore various methods of analyzing local congregations. In addition to providing survey information and data collection procedures, this text looks at the local congregation contextually—its sociological, anthropological, and demographic characteristics.

Waymire, Bob, and C. Peter Wagner. *The Church Growth Survey Handbook.* Milpitas, CA: Global Church Growth, 1984.

A practical how-to book on doing church growth research. It shows the process for collecting data, plotting charts and graphs, and interpreting the information. This is an excellent tool for doing growth charts and provides good diagnostic information.

Education

Collins, Marva. *Marva Collins' Way.* New York: St. Martin's Press, 1982.

A prescription for effective teaching and a graphic indictment of what's wrong with much of American education today. Collins's conviction is that any child can learn. It was her constant "you can do it" that convinced her students there wasn't anything they couldn't accomplish. However, the book is more than just an account of one teacher's struggles and successes; it demonstrates a teaching technique that can be applied in every classroom and home.

Cross, Patricia K. *Adults As Learners.* San Francisco: Jossey-Bass, 1981.

A look at adult education for these times. Cross contends that the adult learner is often neglected in books on higher education. She cites statistics indicating that adult learners are much older than customarily thought and that lifelong education should be emphasized more in the marketplace. She also discusses how adults learn and examines several models of adult learning theory.

Freire, Paulo. *Pedagogy of the Oppressed.* New York: Continuum, 1990.

> An account of how the author, banished from his country by the Brazilian government, traveled abroad to other Two Thirds World countries and developed a theory of education for illiterate peasants. Freire postulates that peasants can learn and critically look at their world and reflect on issues of economic justice and oppression. He therefore suggests that educational methodology for the poor and oppressed must move from a "banking" concept, where the teacher deposits instruction, to a liberation concept, where the teacher empowers the student.

Jones, James M. "Educating Black People for Liberation and Collective Growth." *New Roads to Faith* (September 1972): 3–19.

> An African-American psychologist's look at how blacks and whites interact. He also explores how blacks can better their situation, financially, socially, and economically. He recommends that the black church becomes active as a supplement to public education. The church must also be a facilitator of community awareness.

Kozol, Jonathan. *Savage Inequalities.* New York: Crown, 1991.

> An examination of the consequences of the poor and the oppressed receiving less funding in education than their suburban neighbors. Kozol explores several city school systems, including East St. Louis, New York, and Chicago, and documents the deficiencies of education in these systems particularly in comparison with nearby suburban schools. He contends that the quality of education is in direct relationship to financial distribution by the powers that be.

Lickona, Thomas. *Education for Character.* New York: Bantam Books, 1991.

> An appeal for teaching children respect and responsibility within a public school context. Lickona's basic premise is that morals and values are a missing ingredient and that teaching them in a pluralistic society is not only controversial but almost impossible. He suggests a twelve-point program that offers practical strategies designed to create a working coalition of parents, teachers, and students for teaching character development and responsibility within the school.

Schipani, Daniel S. *Religious Education Encounters Liberation Theology*. Birmingham: Religious Education Press, 1988.

A study that essentially amplifies the methods of Paulo Freire in juxtaposing religious education and liberation theology through dialogue. Schipani suggests that religious education can learn from liberation theology about the practical outworking of education, particularly in the base ecclesial community, and that liberation theology can learn from religious education in terms of content.

Woodson, Carter G. *The Mis-Education of the Negro*. Trenton, NJ: Africa World Press, 1990.

A look at how black people have been educated in the manner prescribed by their oppressors—an education at best inferior and at worst brainwashing. Carter believes that through this mis-education black people have been conditioned to be subservient to whites, to "know their place" in relation to white society.

Missions

Costas, Orlando E. *Christ outside the Gate*. Maryknoll, NY: Orbis Books, 1989.

Several provocative essays that address the issue of missions from a Third World perspective. Costas argues for justice, compassion, and liberation. He views the United States as a mission field for Third World Christians and views the poor and the oppressed as both the object and the subject of missions.

Guinness, Os. *The American Hour*. New York: Free Press, 1993.

A brilliant analysis of the causes of the current moral malaise. Guinness examines how perilously close we have come to losing the shared beliefs, traditions, and ideals that have helped shape America's moral and cultural orders. He also sets forth a compelling view of a new and vital role for American religion in the new millennium and postulates a vision of a restored shared philosophy that allows us to solve the thorny practical questions of living with our deepest differences.

Shaul, Richard. *Heralds of a New Reformation*. Maryknoll, NY: Orbis Books, 1985.

A careful examination of Christian base communities in the light of scriptural and theological resources. Shaul relates the story of the base communities from a Protestant perspective, indicating how they are imaging a new form of church and society. He discusses the implication of the "new reformation" for the North American Christian community.

Social Ministry

Holland, Joe, and Peter Henriot. *Social Analysis.* Maryknoll, NY: Orbis Books, 1983.

The question of how to link the Christian faith to social justice. The authors explore the science of social analysis, looking at the institutions and structures that construct social policy. They deal here more with praxis than with theory.

Sunday School

Banks, Melvin E. "The Black Sunday School: Its Strengths, Needs." *Christianity Today* 8, no. 20 (July 5, 1974): 8–11.

A look at the strengths and needs of the Sunday school for black people. In an article that is dated but instructive, Banks contends that Sunday school curriculum does not represent or meet the need of black churches for educational materials. He views the black church as essential for educating black people and the Sunday school as a crucial vehicle in the educational process.

Birchett, Colleen, editor. *Biblical Strategies for a Community in Crisis.* Chicago: Urban Ministries, 1992.

Inspirational messages and warnings by eleven leading Christian thinkers in the African-American community. Each author reflects on a pressing issue—such as black male role models, the black church, and addictions—and offers positive biblical solutions to each one.

Lynn, Robert W., and Elliot Wright. *The Big Little School.* Birmingham: Religious Education Press, 1971.

The authors discuss the history of Sunday school movement to the present.

Urban Studies

Bobo, Kimberley. *Lives Matter: A Handbook for Christian Organizing*. Kansas City: Sheed and Ward, 1986.

An exploration of world hunger and how Christians can organize to fight against it. Bobo addresses questions of advocacy, lobbying, and coalition building to bring the problem of hunger before the political powers that be.

Conn, Harvie, editor. *Urban Mission* 8, no. 4 (March 1991).

An issue devoted to the tools of urban research. Several articles examine the benefits of collecting data and surveying a community. The article by Judith E. Lingenfelter on ethnographic mapping is particularly helpful. This issue also includes several case studies with statistical data that were collected and put to use by a local church to serve its community.

_____. *Evangelism: Doing Justice and Preaching Grace*. Grand Rapids: Zondervan, 1982.

A look at the barriers that hinder effective evangelism, all of which can be overcome in a Spirit-enlightened approach to a full-bodied ministry of love and mercy. Conn discusses "righteous deeds" as a neglected but essential aspect of effective ministry. Evangelism is a call to preach the gospel of grace, and it works for justice for the poor and oppressed.

_____. *Eternal Word and Changing Worlds*. Grand Rapids: Zondervan, 1984.

The case for the need of a radical reevaluation of Western models for theology and missions. The rise of non-Western and non-white theologies and the changes in understanding of language, culture, and religions force us to realize the inadequacy of ethnocentric, abstracting approaches to theology and missions. Conn informs white evangelical Christians of the need to understand the effect of dialogue between theology, anthropology, and missions for evangelism.

_____. *The American City and the Evangelical Church*. Grand Rapids: Baker, 1994.

Through history and social analysis, an appeal for the evangelical church in America to reconnect with the city. Conn shows how at the turn of the twentieth century the city was the target of the church for evangelism, but as the city took on a negative stereotype, the evangelical church withdrew to the suburbs and largely withdrew from this important mission field.

Conn, Harvie, editor. *Reaching the Unreached*. Phillipsburg, NJ: Presbyterian and Reformed, 1984.

An exploration by nine contributors as to how to identify specific "people groups" and the methods and resources necessary for reaching each of them.

Evans, Anthony T. *Are Blacks Spiritually Inferior to Whites?* Wenonah, NJ: Renaissance Productions, 1992.

A book that addresses an ancient myth in American religious life and argues that the black church has a rich spiritual tradition. While making the case for spiritual equality and racial unity within the body of Christ, Evans describes the distinctives that have made the black church the clearest model of biblical Christianity in the history of America.

_____. *America's Only Hope*. Chicago: Moody Press, 1990.

A statement built on the premise that the church—the body of Christ—holds the key to America's social problems. Evans prescribes a proactive role for the church in engaging the society with moral force. He believes that for too long the church has taken a passive stance toward the larger community and that this has allowed society to morally decay. He believes that a proactive church can make a difference in the United States.

Farnell, Richard. "Through Powerlessness: Engaging Christian Commitment With Urban Reality." *Urban Mission* 7, no. 3 (January 1990): 15–24.

A call for the church to stand with the poor and oppressed in their cry for justice. Farnell contends that the church must side with the powerless against the powerful who seek to oppress.

Fitzpatrick, Joseph P. *Paul: Saint of the Inner City*. New York: Paulist Press, 1990.

A look at the apostle Paul's journeys to the cities of the Mediterranean world in the first century, during which he had to face many of the kinds of problems and trials that confront inner-city ministries today, such as homeless people, poor people, and violence. Fitzpatrick also explores how Paul handled stress, burnout, and lukewarm followers.

Frangipane, Francis. *The House of the Lord.* Lake Mary, FL: Creation House, 1991.

A book described best in its subtitle: "God's Plan to Liberate the City from Darkness." Frangipane holds that God has a plan to solve the moral decay, crime, and drug problems that plague cities. He believes the answer lies in the church—that is, if churches within a city would put aside their differences and doctrinal disputes and develop an urban agenda, the darkness over the city could turn into light. He contends that it takes a citywide church to win a citywide war.

Grant, George. *Bring in the Sheaves.* Atlanta: American Vision Press, 1985.

A study of the question of poverty and how the church has a major responsibility to supply assistance to the poor. Grant contends that the government does not have the ability to resolve the problem of poverty and that private initiatives are more effective.

Greenway, Roger S., editor. *Discipling the City.* Grand Rapids: Baker, 1979.

A look at the city from all angles and directions as the nine contributors address the problems and offer solutions to doing ministry in the urban crucible. They analyze urban ministry theologically, sociologically, and anthropologically. All the writers focus on the city as a prime target for Christian ministry and disciple making.

Gulick, John. *The Humanity of Cities.* Granby, MA: Bergin and Garvey, 1989.

A refreshing new introduction to urban societies that challenges the commonly held view that cities are entirely impersonal, insecure, and disorganized environments in which to live. The author refutes Louis Wirth's arguments set forth in his famous essay "Urbanism as a Way of Life." Combining major urban theories with empirical studies from around the world, Gulick offers poignant glimpses into urban life and shows how its problems are more a result of worldwide forces than the intrinsic nature of cities.

Hessel, Dieter. *Social Ministry.* Philadelphia: Westminster Press, 1982.

The "how" and the "why" of social ministry for a local church. Hessel believes that every church member shares a moral obligation to get involved in the social affairs of its community in order to bring the oppressed out of their captivity. He gives practical suggestions for community organization, networking, and altering social policy.

Kaufman, Gerald, editor. *A Cry for the Cities.* New York: Logos Bible College, 1982.

A collection of several essays that address pertinent topics of urban church ministry. The essays focus on the local church and the tremendous opportunities for ministry in an urban setting, dealing with topics such as prison ministry, discipleship, men's ministry, and Christian education.

Leman, Nicholas. "The Origins of the Underclass I." *Atlantic Monthly* (June 1986): 31–55.

A provocative essay that explores the sociological and historical causes of ghettoization of the urban underclass. The author asserts that the underclass emerged out of the flight of middle-class blacks from urban centers, leaving a disastrously isolated underclass formed less by welfare or lack of jobs than by its rural southern heritage.

_____. "The Origins of the Underclass II." *Atlantic Monthly* (July 1986): 54–68.

A companion essay that explores how to reverse the process of ghettoization through several means, from community development to government intervention.

Meeks, Wayne A. *The First Urban Christians.* New Haven: Yale University Press, 1983.

An exploration of the historical setting of first-century Christians. Meeks recreates the struggle of the early Christians against the

Greco-Roman culture and shows how Christianity was a uniquely urban phenomenon.

Olley, John W. "God's Agenda for the City." *Urban Mission* 8, no. 1 (September 1990): 4–23.

A very positive view of the city that sees it becoming a place of security and justice. Olley examines cities in biblical times and notes that they were places of good as well as evil. He views God's intention as moving from a garden in Genesis to the holy city, the New Jerusalem.

Pannell, William. *Evangelism from the Bottom Up.* Grand Rapids: Zondervan, 1992.

An appeal for urban evangelism based on the premise that "the world is going urban" and "evangelism cannot be separated from ethics." Pannell contends that too much of what is called evangelism has no relationship to justice or to the plight of the oppressed.

Perkins, John. *Let Justice Roll Down.* Ventura, CA: Regal Books, 1976.

The remarkable story of a man who was born the son of a share-cropper, at one time was almost beaten to death, and is now a leading voice for justice. Through his story Perkins challenges the church to work for justice and righteousness.

_____. *With Justice for All.* Ventura, CA: Regal Books, 1982.

The case for a program based on what Perkins calls the three R's: relocation, reconciliation, redistribution. This book is a challenge to white people to overcome guilt for their past and to black people to take responsibility for their future.

_____. *Beyond Charity.* Grand Rapids: Baker, 1993.

A challenge to the church to reach into the city with more than charity and with a gospel that brings wholeness to hurting people. Perkins calls on inner-city churches to work for community development.

Pierce, Augustine F. Gregory. *Activism That Makes Sense.* Chicago: ACTA Publications, 1984.

A "street-wise" explanation of the principles of community organization as they apply to a local church. The author argues that it
is perfectly legitimate for a congregation to act in their self-interest,
to engage in community affairs, and to struggle for those who have
no voice.

Recinos, Harold J. *Jesus Weeps*. Nashville: Abingdon Press, 1992.

The view that North American Christians have begun developing
a global perspective on issues related to the practice of faith in the
world. Their efforts have placed them in solidarity with the justice
and human rights struggles of the Third World. Even so, Recinos
says, the globalization movement has often overlooked the poor
of the First World who are overwhelmingly rooted in the inner
cities. Recinos believes that the world has come to the city and that
the church must seize the opportunity for action.

_____. *Hear the Cry!* Louisville: Westminster Press, 1989.

A candid look at a young Latino pastor's journey from street life,
drugs, and poverty to finding Jesus Christ. This book explores his
calling to the ministry and his struggle to be obedient to God in an
urban setting. The author issues a challenge to the church to be
more robust in her outreach to the poor and the oppressed.

Rogers, Donald B., editor. *Urban Church Education*. Birmingham:
Religious Education Press, 1989.

A comprehensive look at religious education in the urban context,
which the author feels has attracted little attention. The book con-
siders the basic principles, underlying problems, helpful research
data, successful programs, and innovative practices in one of the
most neglected areas in Christian education. Rogers provides a
clear analysis of the complexities and possibilities of urban church
education.

Rorth, Robert E., editor. *Special Ministries for Caring Churches*.
Cincinnati: Standard Publishing, 1986.

A collection of articles on various ministries in which the church
can be engaged. Rorth contends that the church has a responsibility to the sick, the poor, and the elderly and offers practical guidelines in establishing hospice, prison, and crisis pregnancy
ministries, to name a few.

Rose, Larry L., and C. Kirk Hadaway. *An Urban World.* Nashville: Broadman Press, 1984.

A compilation of articles on various topics exploring how the church can contribute positively to the cause of the gospel in urban areas. It offers a look at past, present, and possible future efforts in urban ministry.

Ryan, William. *Blaming the Victim.* New York: Vintage Books, 1976.

A look at how and why society prefers to place the blame for poverty on its victims rather than on the inequalities of American society. The book is a powerful polemic that persuasively articulates a cogent defense for the poor and the oppressed in the United States and argues that inequalities and structural factors are not ordinarily taken into account in discussions of poverty.

Schaller, Lyle E. *Center City Churches.* Nashville: Abingdon Press, 1993.

A book confronting the conventional myth that inner cities do not sustain large churches. Schaller profiles fourteen striving inner-city churches to see how they achieved their success. He also looks at thirty recurring themes among those churches.

Short, John R. *The Humane City.* New York: Basil Blackwell, 1989.

The view that although most people in the Western world live in the city, the structures that make up their dwelling have been developed by people living outside the city. Short shows how the city is often designed not for the poor, but for city planners who have a suburban orientation. He contends that urban dwellers must become proactive in demanding a better quality of life in the city.

Teaford, Jon C. *The Twentieth-Century American City.* Baltimore: Johns Hopkins Press, 1986.

A look at the perceptions of urban problems and the search for solutions from the turn of the twentieth century through the present. Teaford explores the promise of a better life the city offers in comparison with the rigors of agrarian life. However, he documents how the promise of the city has created unrealistic expectations and how vice, overcrowding, and poverty have become the reality of urban life.

Van Houten, Mark E. *God's Inner-City Address*. Grand Rapids: Zondervan, 1988.

An account of the author's experience as an urban missionary in Chicago. Van Houten offers a challenge to Christians to take seriously their responsibility to the homeless and street people. He offers practical and sound advice in crossing the boundaries from middle-class religion to an understanding of God's grace among people of poverty and of ethnic diversity.

Wilson, Bill. *Whose Child Is This?* Altamonte, FL: Creation House, 1992.

An account of the author's life from abandoned child to a pastor in Brooklyn who has developed a powerful ministry for children, touching the lives of 11,000 children off the streets of New York every week. The book addresses issues about Christian education in an urban environment.

Wilson, Ron. "Momma When We Goin' Home?" *World Vision* (April-May 1989): 4–9.

A discussion of the reality of homelessness and its impact on children and women. The author assesses that the homeless problem is becoming more pervasive, with children increasingly at the center.

Zalent, Kim. *Economic Home Cookin'*. Chicago: Community on Economic Development, 1988.

An action guide for congregations committed to community economic development. Zalent addresses topics such as creating jobs, activism, organizing the community, and developing networks with other community groups. The book is filled with practical suggestions and sample forms.